The Design and Evaluation of Public Library Buildings

Nolan Lushington and James M. Kusack

Library Professional Publications
1991

All rights reserved. First published as a
Library Professional Publication, an imprint
of The Shoe String Press, Inc., Hamden,
Connecticut 06514.

Printed in the United States of America.

Library of Congress Cataloging-in-Publication Data:
Lushington, Nolan, 1929–
    The design and evaluation of public library buildings /
Nolan Lushington and James M. Kusack.

        p.   cm.
    Includes bibliographical references and index.
    1. Library architecture.   2. Public libraries—Evaluation.
3. Library buildings.   I. Kusack, James M. (James Michael)
II. Title.

Z679.L95   1991   91-8009
727'.8—dc20

ISBN 0-208-02300-3

Contents

Acknowledgments

My wife Louise Blalock has been of invaluable assistance in talking and thinking about libraries. My library clients and architects are continual sources of challenging inspiration in developing design ideas.

A wide variety of very specific contacts led me to the concept of relating building planning to library roles. Eleanor Jo Rodger's determined Public Library leadership, Charlie Robinson's focus on developing the popular library role, Frank Hemphill's and Karen Ribnicky's designs for display, Douglas Zweizig's talks on output measures, and two decades operating one of the world's busiest public libraries in the remarkably responsive library community of Greenwich, Connecticut all contributed to the planning process described in this book.

Dr. James Kusack's enthusiasm, energy and hard work on the building evaluation process made possible the realization of an idea that had been germinating since I first read about post occupancy evaluation in an American Institute of Architects publication in 1980.

Introducing a new process for planning is obviously full of risks. I am persuaded by Woody Allen's theory "If you're not failing now and again its a sign that you're playing it safe". Building planning by roles and output measures relates so closely to user needs that it is inevitable. This book as a first push in that direction, follows directly from my earlier perspective of designing for users.

—*Nolan Lushington*

Part I

Planning and Design

1

Library Planning

It is now over ten years since the publication of *Libraries Designed for Users* (Library Professional Publications, 1980). That book was an effort to establish the primacy of user satisfaction as the central guide to good library design. It continues to be a useful resource for building planners. Subsequently the number of libraries designed to emphasize user convenience and to de-emphasize barriers such as the monumental, confrontational circulation desk have greatly increased. Information/reference service areas have become the focus of library plans. However, it is time now to revise that practical how-to-do-it guide and, at the same time, to issue this new volume emphasizing the planning process and introducing James Kusack's coordinated evaluation process.

Library user emphasis as a revolutionary trend in public library management has been firmly established by publications about the library planning process and planning and role setting for public libraries by the American Library Association (ALA). These publications use service delivery rather than materials warehousing as the focus for planning.

OUTPUT MEASURES AND PLANNING AND ROLE SETTING

These last publications have introduced a framework that could be useful in the building planning process. The *Checklist of Library Design Con-*

siderations, issued by the Building Section of the Library Administration Division of ALA, also provides a useful tool for library planning.

We are attempting in this work to suggest a comprehensive planning/ evaluation process that will be a model for developing libraries designed for users. This new process attempts to link planning and evaluation into a single cohesive continuum that will motivate library planners to pay attention to user and staff needs by indicating at the outset that there will be an evaluation by users and staff of how well their needs have been met. This process may include expert evaluation based on a professionally prepared design checklist.

The cycle of planning and evaluation with a variety of inputs from community, staff, and expert sources will assure responsible accountability and result in an emphasis on functional design.

In Connecticut, the state library under Richard Akeroyd has taken the leadership in creating a multifaceted process for the improvement of library design, including:

- Matching funds for library construction
- An application process including basic requirements for planning and programming
- Standards for library building planning
- A library space planning guide
- Library planning workshops
- Library interior design workshops
- A post-occupancy evaluation manual
- A building consultant retained by the state library to assist in library planning
- Libra-Tects meetings for architects, librarians, trustees, and community funding and planning agencies to visit new and renovated libraries and review their planning process in order to learn how the do's and don'ts of library building planning actually affect outcomes.

We hope that in the future post-occupancy evaluation will become a state mandated and funded part of the library planning and building process. When this occurs, public libraries will become the leaders in public accountability for capital construction spending, demonstrating administrative and management leadership in a unique manner.

Given these planning assumptions:

The traditional notion based on the democratic assumption that towns of equal population should have equal access to library services is appropriate and should be retained;

That community objectives, library roles, and library use should have some effect on the public library building planning process. How should the process work?

In outline form here is a suggested sequence.

THE LIBRARY PLANNING PROCESS

1. The staff and consultant look around at the community to be served. They collect information about community changes that have taken place since the last library building upgrade.

   Has the population grown?

   Have traffic patterns changed?

   Have community shopping patterns changed?

   Have educational and economic status changed?

   Have there been other significant demographic shifts?

2. The staff and consultant look at library use since the last building upgrade.

   Has circulation increased?

   Has in-library use increased?

   Has reference use increased?

   Has program use increased?

   Have new services or materials been introduced?

3. The consultant evaluates the library building.

   Are the bookstacks filled?

   Are seats often fully occupied?

   Are electrical circuits overloaded?

   Is the parking lot filled?

4. The consultant interviews users and staff to determine their needs. Use focus groups, random intercept interviews, and staff interviews for this information.

5. The staff investigates likely changes in the community for the next twenty years.

6. The consultant estimates library technology change during the next twenty years.

7. The staff and consultant determine how many books and seats are needed by a community of this size for the next twenty years.

Should these quantities be increased because of more intensive use or ambitious objectives, or should these quantities be reduced because of lower use and economic constraints?

8. Staff and trustees set library role priorities and building objectives.
9. The library staff and consultant compile, based on this information, a detailed list of library facility needs: the library program.
10. Consultant and architect work together to assign space requirements to satisfy library service objectives and staff facility needs.
11. Consultant and architect work together to analyze and compare potential sites.
12. Consultant prepares final program recommending functional spaces, sizes, furniture, equipment, and juxtapositions.
13. Consultant and architect work together on schematic planning and drawings.
14. Staff, trustees, consultant, and architect review schematics as they relate to program requirements.
15. Architect develops preliminary plans and cost estimates.
16. Consultant, architect, interior designer, and staff select furniture and equipment, lighting, and graphics.
17. Architect prepares working drawings and construction documents.
18. The staff compares alternatives: construction manager, general contractor.
19. Architect and library staff put plans out to bid, analyze bids, and evaluate contractors.
20. Architect supervises contractor in the construction of the building.
21. Architect and library staff prepare punch list of construction deficiencies.
22. Library staff, consultant, and architect conduct post-occupancy evaluation one year or more after building has been used by the public.

2

General Concepts in Design: Order and Freedom

FREEDOM AND ORDER

Public libraries may be the ideal form of education in a democratic culture because they serve the needs of individuals learning independently at a time of their choice to get what they want from the entire body of recorded knowledge. A. S. Neill in *Summerhill* showed that education requires patience and an environment in which the student chooses the right moment for learning to take place. Librarians and other planners need to seek designs in their buildings that symbolize the offer of a convenient, attractive, and varied opportunity for choice to each individual. To paraphrase Neill: the challenge is to make the library fit the user. Maria Montessori has shown us that order facilitates learning; that children who keep their toys neatly enjoy them more. Libraries dealing with large quantities of materials must organize them in an orderly sequence.

DESIGN PARADOX

This is the paradox in design that librarians and architects must strive to solve: to maintain order while offering variety; to control space and its content while letting people use it when and as needed. Libraries offering free and open access to all kinds of information to all kinds of individuals must symbolize in their design this freedom and individuality by creating an environment that works so well that its users can do what they want in it. While school and college libraries are designed to structure the educational experience, the public library has an opportunity to offer a freer alternative by giving each individual a choice of time and subject.

SELF-SERVICE DESIGN

Symbolizing this individual freedom of choice, the library must be designed to offer the maximum impetus toward self-service with the minimum need for staff interference. The benefits of self-service design include increased use and improved staff productivity, the all-important user confidentiality, and user self-determination and self-confidence as a learner. Ivan Ilyich has urged librarians *not* to get in the way of users who want books. This implies fanatical devotion by librarians and other planners to convenient and open access. Every barrier to the collection of materials and equipment must be perceived, anticipated, and removed, whether it be physical or psychological.

How can library buildings meet the need for order while providing opportunity for such individual freedom of choice in use patterns?

Order in library design must be expressed in the logical sequential layout of the large mass of materials that are used less frequently, while *freedom of choice* is expressed and encouraged by the serendipitous display of the small quantity of intensively used new books, and in the varied choice of environments in which to use them—carrels, chairs and tables, lounge seating, benches, floor cushions, study rooms, conference rooms. Order implies the sequencing of materials on the shelves in order to be able to find something easily.

Short-term use demands above all the possibility of rapid location of specific materials. The bookstack is so huge that effort must be made to arrange it in a rigorously uniform manner, with public access catalog terminals interspersed at regular intervals and signs for stack ends, sections, and subject areas to make self-service browsing relatively speedy and easy. Stacks and terminals for location through a computerized catalog must be immediately accessible to all who enter the building, and their sequential orderly arrangement should be the main orienting feature of the user entrance experience.

Long-term use demands a range of choices in use of books and other data once they are located. Users spend a tiny percentage of their library time in bookstacks. The bookstack's only purpose is to make finding books easy; it is therefore confusing and unnecessarily complex to try to make the bookstack a subject of interesting design. Users spend most of their time in chairs, so these are the most important library furnishings. People differ in size, shape, and taste, so library seating areas should provide a diversity of user choices, such as:

Standing reference is the use of reference books that are heavily in demand by many users who consult them briefly. This type of use can be accommodated by shelving books above waist level with work counters built into the shelving.

Newspapers and magazines, also heavily used, require oversized tables and chairs to minimize interference. Noisy page turning may demand acoustical damping. Lounge chairs and low tables encourage a relaxed, casual, comfortable ambience.

Study carrels offer individual spaces that are apt to be greatly in demand for long-term use because they satisfy the human need for privacy and to "own the turf." Many years ago, that most prolific of library consultants, Keyes Metcalf, determined that carrel height was less important for privacy than the requirement that carrel sides go all the way to the front table edge. About fifteen years ago careful experiments reported in the *IES Journal* determined the best carrel lighting came from both sides rather than the back shelf. Ellsworth Mason urged a decade ago that users be in control of lighting placement, but we are only now beginning to see equipment with user-controlled lighting.

Flexibility has always been a library requirement. Back in the 1920s the great library leader from India, S. N. Ranganathan, said that libraries are growing organisms. Growth requires change and such master practitioners of the library building consulting profession as David Kaser and Raymond Holt warned of the perils of inflexible library planning.

Flexible design includes the rigorous requirement for a full 150-pound floor load bearing capacity in all areas to support the weight of books, and a minimum of twenty-five feet between columns to accommodate a simple, open, regularly shaped floor plan.

Library schematic designs should show the next addition to the library.

Library furnishings and equipment budgets should reserve 10 to 20 percent of expenditures for the end of the first year of occupancy, when new user patterns will emerge.

Assuring flexible space to house library functions, although essential, is insufficient to produce spaces that will satisfy the varying specific needs of users.

A recent analysis of public library use listed over fifty ways in which people use the building. At least ten broad categories of use demonstrate that these different kinds of use need careful definition and attention to assure that the architect's design will respond to these varied needs:

- Return borrowed books. Requires detailed design of book return location and after-hours book drop.
- Browse among new books. Requires spot lighting and front cover display of new materials.
- Find an answer to a question. Requires staff and public terminals to access data bases.
- Ask a librarian for help. Requires an array of print and electronic capabilities for staff use.
- Read a newspaper. Requires special racks and oversized tables.
- Read a magazine. Requires back issue storage, index terminals, microreaders, and printers.
- Use microfilm, video-tapes, phonorecords. Requires special equipment and light-controlled locations.
- Make a copy. Requires copy machines, collating tables, trash baskets, scissors, and coin changer.
- Watch a program. Requires room with stacking chairs, acoustical design, loudspeakers, and special ventilation for closely spaced seating.
- Use a video display terminal. Requires detailed work station design and controlled lighting.

The overall concept and public perception of a library can be divided into several alternative options that an architect could discuss with a client:

The library as a place of *refuge* from the distractions of social, political, and psychological storms to the quiet of the library. This idea of the library as a temperature- and light-controlled environment, independent of the harshness of the natural environment outside, can be very attractive in New England on a cold winter afternoon or in the Midwest on a boiling hot summer day, and the idea of the building as underground cave with delightful environmental conditions inside but completely protected from the weather should be emphasized.

The library as part of the outdoor *environment* is a much more difficult affect to achieve. Libraries built in the 1950s and 1960s surrounded courtyards with natural plantings, washing the windows with heat or cold to temper the atmosphere inside. Perhaps this could be accomplished in the energy conservation age by carefully emphasizing peep-hole windows that would provide eye-level views to people from a sitting position so they could see out into carefully selected garden areas.

The library environment as an *invitation*. This is accomplished in city areas by glass windows that tempt the pedestrian going by to come inside. Perhaps the idea of the kind of sidewalk superintendent peep-hole window is more exciting to people than large masses of glass. Some peep holes, instead of providing a vision into the library, can provide a slide show or; occasionally, a film program or a bulletin board of upcoming library events.

The library as a *symbol* of community education. This concept has traditionally been expressed in a very dignified fashion, with buildings that try to evoke the New England Georgian architectural tradition with red brick and white columns. This is still a very important element in selling buildings to a town board or a library board and certainly expresses a human need to provide continuity with the past and symbols of the library's interest in protecting and preserving traditions. It is very difficult to design a modern functional building that will provide the ambience for the variety of functional library activities inside and still project this severe and formal outside image. Perhaps the kinds of materials selected and the overall shape of the library can evoke some echo of this traditional past without dominating the external structure and making the library seem like an archival town building, rather than the organic, dynamic institution it really is.

The library as an *Eclectic Circus*. This is what really happens in libraries. All the town's citizens young and old, rich and poor—come to the library to satisfy a wide variety of individual intellectual and emotional needs. They can borrow a book, ask a question, find out about community services, decide where to go on vacation, see a film, talk to someone about philosophy, share a cup of coffee with a friend. Children can play a learning game, look at a picture book, listen to a story, go to sleep, find a friend, ask a question. Most importantly, libraries are institutions that individuals can make do what they want, when they want it. Individuals should be able to feel that they control their library experiences and are not controlled by them.

3

Planning for the Future

The "paperless library" has been discussed by F. W. Lancaster and such prophets of the Electronic Age as Ken Dowlin. However, large, recently constructed libraries show minimal understanding of the increasing freedom in library design that the electronic library can bring. We are only beginning to understand that the heart of the library program and its operation must be communication among librarians and library users and the maximum freedom for those users, aided by librarians, to reach into every aspect of our culture and every area of our information base and gain access to every last speck of information they need.

Public library design must recognize that the public use of terminals distributed handily throughout the library will not only help find books in the building but will locate books, periodical information, factual information, and video-tapes from sources inside and outside of the building and help the staff plot a course for user accessibility.

The microterminal is the central feature of design for public and staff and will require movable, adjustable housing alternatives everywhere in the building.

Ken Dowlin, once librarian in Casper, Wyoming, Pike's Peak Library District in Colorado Springs, and now in San Francisco, had a vision of the library of the future as a community information-communication hub. Input would come from a wide variety of community agencies and output would be measured not only by lending books and answering questions, but by the library serving as a central computer bank for access by home computers and by disseminating information through cable programs, meetings, and electronic mail.

F. W. Lancaster, the library futurist, predicts that books will continue to be the major information resource for the general public through 2010, but there are a variety of future trends that may have some impact on library planning well before that date: On-Line Computer Library Center (OCLC) and other bibliographic utilities and inexpensive telefacsimile (fax) technology will have three effects:

1. Libraries will discard little-used materials because they will be quickly accessible from outside the building.
2. Libraries will purchase fewer little-used items for the same reason.
3. Smaller libraries with well-trained staff will be able to obtain items much more easily from remote sources.

Microfiche, CD-ROM, and other optical disc technology will access huge amounts of recently published and intricately indexed materials in a greatly reduced space, but with considerable additional machine work station space and electrical needs. Many of these work stations will require only stand-up access because of the speed of searches and responses.

COMPACT STORAGE

In spite of their limiting public access, high-density compact storage conventional book stacks and industrial automated retrieval systems such as the robotic system envisioned for the California State University Library at Northridge and the new Bibliothèque National will have the advantage that they store little-used books at half the cost in a third of the space needed for conventional stacks. In addition, they improve handicapped access to top and bottom shelves; lower heating, ventilating, and air conditioning costs; and improve shelf sequence because of automated accuracy. Speeding up remote electronic access may eventually eliminate the need for compact storage except in the largest archival libraries.

REVOLUTION OF RISING EXPECTATIONS

Library patrons will come to expect what we in 1990 consider to be miracles of access. They will expect quicker access to more materials from resources outside of the building. Our present interlibrary loans and photocopy requests, now accounting for less than one-tenth of 1 percent of loans will increase to 10 percent, requiring a better-trained and larger staff as well as more automated procedures.

Collection development staff working with automated systems will have an improved understanding of what is in demand and what is unused. Materials will be frequently shifted from high-use to lesser-used storage formats monitored by an integrated automated system. Staff promotion of high-quality materials will be enhanced by improved book review information incorporated into multilevel automated public access catalogs that permit varied search techniques.

Many of the building implications of these trends are self-evident, but they can be clarified and summarized. The late 1990s will witness the coming of age of the service-oriented small library and a reduced emphasis on the materials-oriented library.

Subject orientation of library staff working in large multilibrarian information centers will make a wide range of library services available to every citizen in person or by telephone. Vastly increased bibliographic control and easier, patron-oriented access to materials by a wide variety of computer terminals will also revolutionize service.

MAKING CONVERSIONS

Lancaster has made projections for the conversion of library materials into electronic formats. The sum of his predictions is that the 1990s will see a gradual conversion of scholarly and technical material into electronic formats. At first this conversion will focus on indexes and bibliographic tools, but the introduction of ABI Inform already combines indexing and full text in CD-ROM multiple discs. It is difficult to estimate when this conversion to electronic format will have a major impact on library building planning. However, I predict changes will take place in the following sequence:

1990

Public access computerized catalogs accessed through terminals distributed throughout the library will replace card catalogs.

Public access terminals will access not only the library's holdings but also other holdings in the Local Area Network (LAN), as well as regional holdings.

Public terminals will use an array of CD-ROM databases, including full-text encyclopedias and magazine articles. This will have minimal affect on space requirements except in the area of magazine storage. The building will of course have to be completely wired for many work station terminals. This may be accomplished by installing flat wiring and carpet tile, power poles, Teflon cables for low voltage in the ceiling plenums, fiber optic cables, and power raceways in a floor grid.

1995

Conversion of full text to electronic format and high-resolution screens may require more, larger electronic work stations, perhaps in a mobile flexible pattern of operation.

2000

The continued conversion to electronic format and the existence of high-resolution screens may introduce the single-format library, in which several information delivery systems are combined in a single electronic format: alphanumeric symbols like books, using words and numbers, moving pictures like VCR cassettes, and sound reproduction with CDs.

2010

Electronic Home Delivery enables materials and information to be borrowed from the library or fed into the home electronically through addressable cable systems. This will require cabling and complex but compact electronic devices controlled by reference librarians. This may begin to reduce the need for retrospective storage of hard copy for reference purposes. Librarians preparing for this will need to plan for transmission systems directed from the library information-reference center.

This highly speculative scenario envisions a library with gradually decreasing book storage needs and gradually increasing complex and expensive electronic work stations and cable transmission systems. The constant will be the reference librarian working with the user to achieve control and understanding of the user's needs.

Basically, technology has made it easier to plan by providing an array of technical solutions. Flexible design and detailed planning will continue to be the key to user convenience and staff effectiveness. The basics of power distribution and total wired access are now common places in mechanical design. Librarians and consultants need to assure their application to *library* design solutions by detailing specifications, reiteration in planning meetings, and detailed plan reviews.

Remote or distance learning is currently a hot topic among educators. Public libraries, though not formal educational institutions, have always been interested in cooperating with other educational institutions in support of their programs. In England the Open University System is strongly supported by public libraries. Remote learning provides a unique opportunity for libraries to participate in an open, less structured educational environment well suited to their formal support to education role.

4

Library User Experience
and Traditional Planning

THE LIBRARY EXPERIENCE: THE PRESENT REALITY

You have recently arrived in town and, passing a distinguished-looking building, you decide to visit and see what it has to offer. After finding a parking place several blocks away you climb the twenty-one well-worn granite stairs and enter a vestibule with a soaring ceiling. Off this central space you enter one of the symmetrical side rooms and find it filled with grey steel bookcases. Sitting at a finely carved desk overflowing with papers and draped with electrical cords from a terminal sits a librarian, searching through a large reference file surrounded by piles of books and catalogs. The uncomfortable-looking chairs and tables jammed into a corner sit under a noisily humming and flickering fluorescent light fixture that, with only two of its four lamps lit, competes unsuccessfully with the baking hot sunlight pouring in a tall window partially obscured by more steel bookstacks.

Trying to locate a catalog or terminal to find a book you wander back to the vestibule and across to the other symmetrical room on the other side, where you find a high stacked card catalog with two people waiting to use it. When your turn comes you find your book's number but search in vain for a map to locate it in the building. Checking nearby books and following their sequence you climb to the book balcony only to find it is not the right place. Descending to the catalog you try again, this time back across the hall. Failing a second search you interrupt the librarian to ask for a subject location; you are directed to the basement archive room, but the title you want is not there either.

A 1960s LIBRARY

Determining that the process is not worth the gain you cross town to the new branch. You have parked in a library lot just a few feet from the entrance, and an ugly concrete box allows you to enter without climbing stairs. An information desk and card catalog at the entrance provides a quick location and the single-sequence bookstack leads you quickly to the stack, but your book is not available and repeated searches leave you equally frustrated. The bright glaring lighting, hard-edged formica tables, and modern square chairs leave you without the comfort of good aesthetic feelings. You want to flee this concrete prison and find some sheltering warmth in the old library across town.

PLANNING AND DESIGN

What do these stories tell us about library building planning and design as they relate to services?

- The library building is only a means to an end. Its function is to facilitate the service.
- Library service is people (staff and public) and materials.
- People respond to feelings about buildings as well as to the library building as a tool for finding and using materials.
- Planning a library building must start with an understanding of people's aesthetic needs and the functional requirements of being able to quickly and easily gain access to an increasingly bewildering array of materials and services.

Methodology

The planning process then must provide a methodology for:

- Determining space needs for materials, services, staff, and users. This is done by understanding the traditional standards for public library services and modifying these standards according to community needs and service objectives. This step results in a formal written program of building needs derived from objectives for the library.
- Translating this program into a building plan should be done through an interactive community process with focus groups, architectural forums, and staff discussions modifying the program.

- The architect then begins to develop schematic plans with consultant and staff feedback suggestions guiding but not hampering architectural observations and creative concepts based on present and projected library use patterns.

Population-Based Planning

Over the past fifty years, libraries have been planned in relation to population. The planner first determined population projections for the municipality based on information from town, regional, or state planning authorities or public utilities. Population projections were then applied to empirical library standards derived from prominent library consultants such as Joseph Wheeler. These standards became national and state standards adopted by the American Library Association and state library planning agencies, such as Wisconsin and Connecticut.

Planning Formulas

For example, a town of 20,000 using these standards would build a library capable of seating 100 people (five seats per thousand population) and housing 60,000 to 100,000 books (three to five per capita). To complete the building size, other formulas are used, such as 20 percent of the building for staff work area and 25 percent for nonassignable space for such nonlibrary functions as heating, ventilating, airconditioning, rest rooms, corridors, elevators, stairs, walls, and so forth.

Seating capacity can easily be translated into a space requirement using the architectural formula of twenty-five to thirty square feet per seat, and book capacities could become space requirements depending on types of books, such as seven books per running foot of shelf space for reference and fifteen books per foot for juvenile books.

Some state library agencies, such as the one in Connecticut, have converted capacity standards and space formulas into basic square foot requirements, such as one square foot per capita for libraries serving populations up to 20,000 and a slightly smaller area per capita as the population increases.

Library size is, of course, basically related to population served, but, increasingly, many other factors will affect size, including:

- Community educational levels
- Library use
- Community financial resources
- Other nearby libraries

- Local regional and national library networks
- Other community cultural resources
- Library role objectives
- Private library fund-raising and gifts
- Library staff
- Library management

5

New Planning Methodologies: Library Roles

We believe that public library planning should continue to be based on equal opportunity population formulas. However, the planning process should also focus on community-based user input, library role objectives, and output measures.

Formula sizing is still generally in use but is recently being modified by a new generation of library planners who are beginning to concentrate on community objectives, library roles, and library use.

Library roles differ radically in their effect on design. Size of library buildings will continue to be influenced by population projections but roles will play an increasingly greater part in interior functional design. We will attempt to show in this chapter how library roles and output measures may affect library designs. Library roles as identified by the Public Library Association include popular materials library, reference library, community activities center, community program center, preschoolers door to learning, formal education support center, independent learning center, and research center.

Differences in the use of libraries and even descriptions of the kinds of uses vary widely from town to town and from decade to decade. Uses are difficult to predict and not uniform. In 1972 I visited a dozen recently constructed English libraries and was surprised to find that their circulation per capita was almost double that of similar American libraries. Education is generally considered the most reliable predictor of library use, but exciting library buildings—such as interior designer Marshall Brown's library in Chula Vista, California—can revolutionize library use in a blue-collar town, given the right kind of staff support and leadership of directors such as Rosemary Lane.

Ernest de Prospo and his successors in public library research during the 1970s and 1980s have developed a set of library roles and output measures that can serve as useful design guidelines for library planners.

THE POPULAR LIBRARY ROLE: WHAT USERS WANT

Half the people coming to small- and medium-sized libraries want a book to read. They are not seeking a specific subject or title—just a good, interesting book. In small libraries they primarily want fiction, and many want something new (less than six months old) that they have heard about in a television show, newspaper, or magazine or that a friend recommended. From the staff's point of view, high-demand new books are difficult to supply when needed because of the cost of purchasing sufficient duplicate copies to meet demand.

Sharon (Shay) L. Baker of the University of Iowa School of Library and Information Science has compiled a list, based on research, of what public library users want.

The most popular fiction purchases are genre fiction—especially mystery-suspense, romance, action-adventure, and historical fiction. The most popular nonfiction purchases are of self-help reference materials, followed by humanities and social science titles. Circulation per volume purchased will increase until the collection reaches 100,000 to 125,000 volumes. Circulation studies show that libraries emphasizing popular materials and buying multiple copies of high-demand items tend to have higher circulation per capita rates than libraries that emphasize diversity rather than duplication, even at the expense of failure to satisfy popular demand at its peak.

From a building point of view these books represent a fraction of those owned by the library. Since the library is serving many people with these few books, they should be spread out on display shelves with cover out rather than shelved with spine out. In this display the architect will devote a square foot of area to every five books, while in the bookstack area a square foot will house ten books. In compact high-density storage the density is thirty to forty books per square foot because aisles are reduced by putting stacks on movable tracks.

Best-sellers heavily promoted in the media are of course the materials most in demand. Early in their circulating life they spend very little time on the shelves, since they are on multiple reserve. Later in their useful life they are still in demand and should be displayed right near the circulation desk for quick, convenient turnover. Small slanted dumps or built-in circulation desk holders can best accommodate these high turnover materials.

Since the books are returned and checked out at the circulation desk, that is where the most popular books should be immediately displayed as, in this photo.

Popular new books need to be spread out for browsing ease. Cover-out display will result in the highest rate of circulation. Display choices include:

- Display units with sloping shelves
- Bookstore fixtures, such as pyramids
- Slatwall-end panels or wall units
- Spinners-Towers that are adjustable in height and with interchangeable shelves. Spinners are difficult to sequence

Other equally popular high-intensity use materials should also be in the popular library area. VCR's, CD's and audio books can be displayed on multimedia shelving and theft protected by a bypass theft detection unit.

Seating in this heavy traffic high-use area should be minimal, with stand-up short-term browsing shelves, stools, and benches. Planning for

this space should take into consideration output measures for the popular library role.

Output measures for the popular library include attendance per capita, circulation per capita and browsing fill rate. If these measures exceed norms, more space may be required. It is well to realize that *display shelving* of books tends to increase circulation, thus reducing the space required to house materials.

A library of 100,000 books with 30,000 in circulation requires less space than one with the same size collection but only 10,000 books in circulation. Eighty percent of people coming into the library want the 20 percent of the library's books most in demand. Twenty percent of library patrons are interested in the remaining 80 percent of the library's holdings. Therefore, the high-demand materials sought by the largest number of users should be spread out on display shelving, while the remaining 80 percent can be housed in standard or perhaps even high-density stacks.

Frank Hemphill in Baltimore County, Maryland, and Dave Smith in Hennepin County, Minnesota, have shown that library use can increase dramatically in a given community with the innovative use of display shelving for books and open access design. Que Bronson in Maryland has spoken forcefully about such simple display techniques as floor displays and cardboard or plastic display dumps.

Design

Details of interior design of library furnishings can affect library use and space requirements. What are some design factors that tend to encourage use?

- Easy browsing: display front covers of materials in large quantities seems essential; spreading out new acquisitions on shelves that are not too high or low; mixed media browsing.
- Dramatic spot lighting in high-use areas with increased emphasis on browsing shelves. The Metropolitan Museum of Art book store in New York recently introduced spot lighting *below* eye level using the new capsylite lamps.
- Immediate access to materials at the library entrance.
- Concealing entrance barriers, such as check-out desks, and theft detection units so they are evident as you leave, not as you enter.
- Immediate access to a knowledgeable people-oriented staff, not to the book monitoring staff.

- Children's book and story areas visible as part of the library experience.
- Video and audio cassettes immediately available for loan.
- Comfortable seats with support for back and shoulders.
- All materials on one floor.
- Easy-to-follow arrangement sequence for books; books arranged uniformly in Dewey decimal sequence.
- Self-service graphics coordinated with maps and flyers, Dewey locator system, and clear explanations of subject number.
- A central staff service location, with several staff members clearly available for assistance.
- Staff-public data terminals conveniently located throughout the building.
- Staff work area adjacent to public service areas.
- Reference materials near staff public service locations.

Browsing

A sample program for the browsing area of a small popular library serving five thousand people might read as follows:

The browsing area should contain a selection of ever-changing materials, including current magazines, paperbacks, a choice of art and general interest picture books, recently returned materials, a new book browsing section, and a popular collection for young adults. Video cassettes, audio cassettes, and CD's will be here also. Wall shelving with task lighting and sloping display shelves will impart a warm and inviting atmosphere, conducive to wanting what one sees, to this part of the library. Arrangement should be informal and attractive, with low-key lighting emphasizing the materials. Furnishings and colors should be elegant, comfortable, and relaxing. A person entering this part of the library should get the same feeling as in a lively book store with a variety of materials readily available for use in the building or to check out. Colors in this area should not compete with books and pictures; use warm earth tones.

Free-standing furnishings in this area will be lower than 46 inches to give an open, uncluttered appearance. Racks for hard-and softcover books should permit views of front covers and spines (see illustration). This area should contain comfortable durable seating with support for lower back and shoulders. Magazine display for fifty titles has storage underneath for one year of back issues, and there should be one thousand books, CD's, and videos.

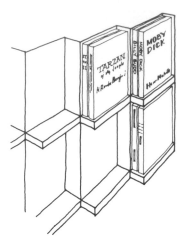

Paperback book rack permitting view of spine *and* front cover.

Book capacities for the popular library need to be greatly expanded. At present most libraries display less than 1 percent of their collection and often devote less than 1 percent of their space to this vital and popular function. Five percent or more might be a more reasonable space allocation, recognizing that books displayed in this manner will require one square foot of space for five books rather than ten to fifteen books.

Some recently designed libraries are extending book display techniques into their general stack areas by using one or more of the following techniques:

- No books shelved lower than 10 inches or higher than 60 inches
- Large format oversized books displayed at eye level-48 inches
- Zig zag shelf inserts for display on every other section
- Extra wide 48-inch aisles.

These methods will either result in larger stack areas or smaller stack capacities than conventional shelving, but book circulation will increase.

Audio-Visual Services

Modern public libraries include many different formats and types of information. They are no longer just places for books or magazines. Video and audio cassette services are the most rapidly growing of library services, frequently characterized by a high-intensity use of relatively small collections. This has resulted in such aberrations as having cassettes at a staff service area and requiring the public to browse in the empty boxes.

As we enter the 1990s these collections will expand rapidly in size and decrease in unit costs, requiring open stack housing which can be easily protected by the new theft detection systems. These high-intensity-use, rapid turnover materials should be located for quick easy browsing near the circulation service area, where they can be easily supervised.

The materials collected by libraries often include:

- *Videos.* These might include entertainment features, documentaries, and how-to, exercise, travel, or instructional video-tapes.
- *Compact discs,* audio cassettes, records, books on tape, and spoken word recordings.
- *Microforms.* Microfilm and microfiche for back issues of magazines or selected government documents are also very common in public libraries. They are, however, usually housed in the reference area rather than in the audio-visual department.
- *Computer Software.* Microcomputer discs and online data services are increasingly important sources of valuable information in libraries. Like microforms, they are also often located in the reference area, since they are similar to print indexes and other reference books but in machine readable form.

These materials are different from conventional library materials like books, magazines, and newspapers because:

- Machines are needed to use them.
- Machine maintenance is required.
- Users often need instruction.
- In the case of microforms, browsing of the material is less common, users seek specific information.
- Unit cost is often higher than for books.
- Their compact size makes theft easier.
- Materials can be erased when the library uses some kinds of detection systems.

Libraries have adopted various strategies or alternatives for dealing with these kinds of materials. The options include:

- Displaying covers or boxes in a public area while retaining the actual material in a secure area. Library users can then browse the surrogates, locate an item of interest, and request the library staff to deliver the actual materials. This option is time consuming and limited by the amount of secure storage area.

- Interfiling audio-visual materials with books on standard book shelves. This option maximizes browsing but the potential for theft is high. Interfiling is useful for travel video-tapes and books-on-tape, but the scattered access may be discouraging for users seeking a particular format. A possible alternative is cross-signage, reminding browsers in the bookstacks that videos on the subject are also available. Similarly, signs in the video collection could remind browsers of books on that same subject.

- Materials displayed and available to the public in a secure area. Machines to use these materials can be located nearby. This option requires a separate room or area with staff supervision and theft detection devices. It maximizes public access and browsing while protecting valuable library assets. It also limits staff costs. This option may be the best for many libraries.

Design considerations for the audio-visual department include:

- A staff able to supervise access to materials
- A design that permits browsing by the public in a secure area with access through a narrow opening near to a staff service counter
- Machines on carts for ease in replacing and maintaining the equipment
- Adequate electrical outlets for the machines
- Flexible design to allow for shelving and browsing bins that accommodate a variety of formats
- A spread display of recent or popular materials
- Lighting that is directional and oriented toward tasks to avoid glare on CRT monitors

Circulation Area

Crucial to its operations, and one of the library's most active services, is the circulation (loan and return) of books and other materials. The circulation desk is the place where books and other materials are returned. It should be possible to leave materials to be returned conveniently at the circulation desk upon entering the library. This self-service feature will eliminate the necessity of a staff member having to check in books as soon as the patron drops them off. Provision should be made for quick and easy staff check-in of materials.

The circulation desk should include space to help the public and a work area contiguous to the service desk. These should be visible from one another, yet acoustically separated from the rest of the library. The lighting should be task lighting.

Books may be charged out for children at the same circulation desk. One section of the desk will be low enough for children to feel welcome and comfortable. This area will also be useful for persons in wheelchairs.

The circulation desk provides many important service activities besides loans and returns, such as reserves, collection of fines and fees, renewals, photocopy assistance, and answering the telephone. Space is also needed for storage of supply items, bindery and discarded materials, reserves awaiting pick-up, processing returned books and computer terminals.

The circulation desk should be designed to accommodate terminals for an automated circulation system, including cabling for future local area networks. Telephone conduits and dedicated outlets will be installed.

Storage beneath and behind the circulation counter will provide a variety of flexible spaces for forms, books, machines, and supplies. An effort will be made in design to keep the top of the counter clear of clutter and to organize easily accessible compartments for all supplies and materials. There will be ample space behind the service desk for easy and efficient movement of staff and book trucks. A cash register and theft detection equipment may be installed in the area.

The library's circulation control system may require a telephone modem if the library is part of a remote network. A public access catalog

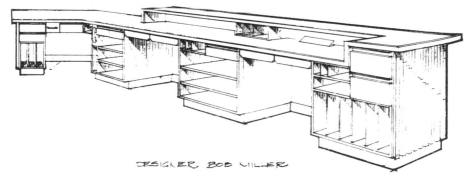

DESIGNER BOB MILLER

A thoughtfully designed circulation counter for adults and children with 39" high transaction top and lower 30" high staff work counter. Machines fit on top of the work counter and underneath the transaction top. (*Groton, Connecticut Library.*) *Designer*: Bob Miller of Lyons, Mather and Lechner.

with public terminals should be considered in the overall design of all services, furnishings, and electrical and telephone wiring.

It is important to identify to the public where various public services, such as check-out and return, are performed. This will be done with appropriate lighted and well-placed graphics.

Dual height circulation service counters provide useful separation of public and staff functions. Future flexibility is assured by modular mobile inserts below the service counter.

Magazines and Newspapers

Popular and reference library roles make extensive use of both magazines and newspapers, so they are a logical transition bridge.

There are two different types of users of newspapers and magazines. One is the casual popular browser who is interested in today's paper or this week's magazine, and the other is the reference user who has looked up the newspaper or magazine in a print, CD-ROM, or online index and wants a number of back issue newspapers or magazines. As online indexes become more current, this reference use involves more recent issues. Thus newspapers and magazines are related to both popular and reference roles of the public library.

Older issues are currently available in several different formats:

- Loose copies often grouped in hanging oblique files or in plastic boxes
- Bound periodicals like books, sometimes in high-density compact stacks, requiring a structural floor load capability of three hundred pounds per square foot
- Microformats such as microfilm or microfiche involving machines, such as microfilm reader-printers, which often require staff assistance
- CD ROM or online terminals that may include index and full text on the same format. Interestingly, these may require only minimal staff assistance since they are self-instructing

Output measures related to magazine and newspaper use include in-library use per capita, reference use per capita, and circulation per capita for circulating copies.

Current magazines and newspapers can be housed with only current issues on a single alphabetical display wall, or with the past six months of older issues on shelves beneath the current display issue. These current issues are high-demand, high-turnover materials and, as such, should be spread out on many front cover display shelves and not concentrated on fewer shelves. Libraries that make more extensive use of magazines than the norm may require additional space for this function.

REFERENCE ROLE

The reference library is the heart of a wide variety of services and the major service center for the interaction of professional librarians and users. Quick and easy access to an ever increasing variety of CD and online terminals will be basic in this area as well as access to the reference book collection, indexes, magazines and the larger nonfiction book collection. For these reasons it should have these characteristics to be considered in planning the building:

- Centrally located
- Visible from entrance
- Near reference and nonfiction books
- Near card catalog and terminals
- Near staff work area or offices

Reading-Study Seating

Recent studies have demonstrated that individuals vary more than they are similar in their requirements for comfortable seating. It is very obvious that the old style reading room with row upon row of identical chairs and tables is an entirely inappropriate reading or reference environment. Instead, a wide choice of different reading spaces should be available, including:

- Individual study carrels with low sides and backs, and ergonomically shaped chairs with curved backs and sides. Adjustable working surfaces and chair seats recognize the need to change working positions during long-term involvement.
- Extra wide tables for newspaper and magazine use.
- Comfortable lounge chairs with lower back lumbar and upper shoulder support provide extra comfort for long-term use.
- Sloping tables to support heavy reference and art books.

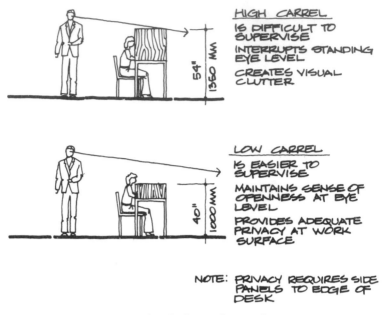

HIGH CARREL
IS DIFFICULT TO SUPERVISE
INTERRUPTS STANDING EYE LEVEL
CREATES VISUAL CLUTTER

54" 1360 MM

LOW CARREL
IS EASIER TO SUPERVISE
MAINTAINS SENSE OF OPENNESS AT EYE LEVEL
PROVIDES ADEQUATE PRIVACY AT WORK SURFACE

40" 1000 MM

NOTE: PRIVACY REQUIRES SIDE PANELS TO EDGE OF DESK

Proper height for study carrels.

INFORMATION SERVICES (reference and reader's advisor)

People use libraries not only for books to read but, equally important, for information they need for satisfactory and productive lives. In some communities, more than half the people who enter library buildings do not borrow books. They read magazines and newspapers, ask questions, look up facts, watch films, attend lectures and concerts, and discuss important issues. As life has become more complex, people have begun to realize the wide variety of information necessary to shape their lives—much of which can be provided by libraries through qualified staff and quality resources.

NO SHOULDER OR LUMBAR SUPPORT

GOOD SHOULDER & LUMBAR SUPPORT

Comparison of lounge chairs.

A library is devoted to satisfying the individual information needs of every citizen. Students from elementary grades through graduate school, as well as independent learner adults, use libraries as an information resource. Users of all ages, particularly adults, seek information on a wide variety of subjects relating to their personal investment planning, gardening, arts and literature, career changes, health problems, crafts, and so forth. Also, many users ask for guidance in their selection of recreational reading, including fiction and nonfiction subject matter.

Information service center design should receive the utmost attention at the schematic phase because of its multiple functions. These functions are central to the library's operation, and it is important that these services center on a single, concentrated, core service area.

The centrally located information center is the main access point for service. It must be convenient to the card catalog or catalog terminals, reference books, and the increasing variety of machines necesary to use the wide range of materials such as microfilm and microfiche reader-printers and computer terminals, in a modern library. It should also be close to the periodical collection.

The information center should consist of a large service counter with standing and sitting places for the staff and the public, shelving for reference books, and files for pamphlets and microfilm. Lighting in this area must be glare free but intense enough for long periods of use with minimal eye fatigue. Since both staff and public will be in this area for long periods of time, climate must be carefully controlled for both temperature and humidity.

Telephone information service is an important aspect of library reference service. To handle telephone service, at least two telephone lines should be installed at the information center. Up to forty percent of all reference inquiries come in by telephone. Expanded adequate quarters with improved telephone system capability may increase this demand. Any service organization requires and relies heavily on its telephone system, and this is especially true of public libraries.

Design

Every new library building and most renovations include a location where the staff meets the public to answer questions and provide other services. Library equipment design has generally treated information desks by adapting furniture designed for other purposes, such as single or double pedestal office desks or circulation counters. Many information desks are custom designed for a particular library and then become obsolete within five years. The user functions that take place at the information desk are as follows:

- Ask questions of the staff. These may require considerable time to define by conversation with the staff member or with more than one staff specialist in a large library. There should be an opportunity for the user to sit down so that conversation takes place at eye level and so that both parties may take notes.
- The user may be given a reference book to consult briefly for an answer and will need to write down a citation from the book for future reference; space for a large book, paper and pen and a person standing up to use them is needed.
- The user may need to consult a CRT terminal that has been manipulated by a staff member or by the user. This will necessitate a locking half-circle turntable with a hollow center for wiring and, if possible, a lowered portion of the work counter, or a double-faced terminal.
- The user will need to fill out a form for materials not immediately available, thus requiring form slots and an explanatory sheet for interloan.
- In order to support user wants the staff will need access to a wide variety but small quantity of materials and devices including several CRTs with glare preventing glass and hoods, a high-speed computer printer with acoustical cover, fifty to one hundred books, vertical files for pamphlets, floppy disk storage to structure computer searches, a manual multicounter to keep track of user statistics, telephone line and acoustic coupler with modem, and microfiche and reader for telephone numbers and college catalogs.
- A single staff member at an information center may well be able to give assistance to several users in various stages of performing complex searches so it will be important to allow for several user spaces for each staff space in busy libaries.

Functional Relationships

Hierarchies of use will dictate which functions of heaviest use, such as those listed below, will be grouped around the information center:

- Magazine and newspaper indexes CD-ROM or bound, with micro materials, readers, and printers
- Heavily used reference books-bibliographies, encyclopedias
- Daily newspapers and current magazines
- Easily supervised compact seating, such as ganged carrels
- Dated business and tax services, especially investment services
- In small-and medium-sized libraries, the entire nonfiction collection

The information center should include the following design characteristics.

- *Flexibility* in work surface height, electrical connections, shelving, and compartmentation to accommodate varying computer terminal sizes and the mix of machines and staff that will be constantly changing in the next ten years. A system design that can be changed by the staff at will is essential. Cantilevered shelves, knock-outs, for wiring and slotted compartments will be necessary.
- *Modularity* for ease of manufacture and replacement will be necessary because of the widely varying size of the library facility. Although three feet is the standard shelf module in America, metric sizing should be considered for the future.
- *Knee space* for the public as well as staff should be made available by removing cantilevered shelves and compartments.
- *Form wells* spaced and grouped with slotted sides and zig zag bottoms will be helpful to organize forms, pencils, counters, and other necessary impedimenta and clutter.
- *Side file drawers or wells* with pendaflex files are nothing new, but it is surprising how seldom they are found in this part of the library and how essential they are for rapid access to files.
- *Wiring boards and circuit breakers* for telephone and electrical connections easily made and changed will be essential for quick change and trouble shooting in this area.
- *Transaction height work counters* for staff-public interaction and lower height shielded area for staff-only use are requirements.

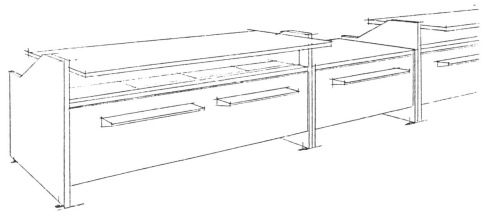

Jens Risom design.

THE COMMUNITY INFORMATION CENTER

This role is closely related to the reference function. Automation of community information and its integration with personal computer terminals available remotely or at the library as part of the library's On Line Public Access Catalog (OPAC) or Local Area Network (LAN) may require space for additional staff and public terminals.

THE RESEARCH LIBRARY

This role of the public library may require additional compact high density material storage space (300 pound live load structural capacity) or even robotic storage for those infrequently accessed but unique items of unusual or local interest. These rare materials may require special humidity/temperature control and staff-only controlled access.

THE CHILDREN'S LIBRARY ROLE: PRESCHOOLERS DOOR TO LEARNING

Until recently children's departments in libraries were the stepchildren of library design, often looking like smaller versions of the table and bookstack school of library design.

However, at Dallas, Texas; Cerrito, California; and in several other recently designed libraries there is beginning to be an acknowledgement that children's areas should reflect differences in use, size, and approaches to books and a multitude of other media.

For a child, the first visit to the public library should be a magical first contact with an amazing variety of vicarious experiences. For children used to the glamor and excitement of television and the wonderful world of theme parks, the library must offer a different but equally imaginative environment.

Some characteristics that should be considered for the children's environment include:

- The individual child's ability to select from a wide array of books and media the one he or she wants most is the strongest element distinguishing the library from other institutions in children's experience. This ability to choose has the inherent danger that the choice may be inappropriate—too difficult, boring, dull, or easy.
- Assisting the child in choosing or finding requires both a self-

service and self-instructing environment, as well as quick and easy access to supportive librarians.

- Building requirements include shelving types appropriate to easy choice, such as low picture book bins to make it easy for children to select from the front covers of books.
- Special small box shelving for smaller format books as well as low divider shelving for tall format books should be available.
- A central staff station with staff work area near the entrances and a browser location will assure staff help when necessary.
- Videos, audio cassettes on spinners, or low displays near preview machines will link access to viewing.
- Imaginative housing for books, such as large bolt-together display boxes such as in the Gressco Modul-A system, book houses as at the Dallas Public Library, enchanted book forests, and surprises linking book subjects and environments should encourage children to explore new subjects.
- Different-sized furnishings to accommodate children of a variety of sizes and shapes. Seating for them must include four size differences. There should be sloping picture book tables, cubby corners, platform perches, carpeted cubes, foot-high floor cushion tables, as well as miniature rockers and large toys.
- Computers with carefully planned adjustable work stations in high-tech space capsule housings, nearby software and self-instructing learning modules should let children's imaginations soar.
- Story hour is a wonderful tradition in children's rooms. This area should be acoustically separated from study areas, have lighting on dimmers, and an array of media equipment, in addition to stepped-up carpeted platforms for audience and performers. Puppet show facilities should also be provided.

Children's responses to a variety of designs and services has never been seriously studied. A recent interview with a rural children's librarian produced an interesting finding. Recognizing the need to keep picture books in alphabetical order to make searching for a title easier, the library included divider-type low conventional picture book shelving. However, as the picture book collection increased and began to run out of shelf space, the librarian decided to order enough low picture book browsing bins to house the A-D section of picture books. Much to her surprise, she found that these books circulated at a

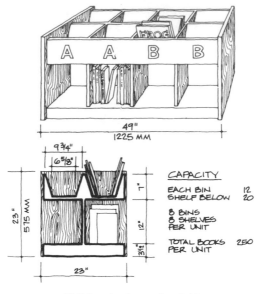

Children's picture book bins.

400 percent greater rate than the E-Z picture books on the conventional shelving. Over a period of several years she gradually increased the picture book bins, finding that as she did it the children had rediscovered these other picture books. Forced to choose between order and use, she chose use.

Increasing use of computers by children, their receptivity to change and flexibility in formats and space, as well as the variety of shapes, sizes, and styles in children point to the adoption of four distinct concepts in children's libraries that reflect the concepts of order and freedom.

- *Order* expressed in bookstacks interspersed with display points for front cover display of subjects together with supergraphic Dewey numbers.
- *Freedom* to move furniture points to the need for sturdy light weight chairs and tables and mobile work stations in an open free-form area.
- *Platforms* to offer small children an opportunity to climb to a higher space and perch there to read or look at the other children below.
- *Quiet* work stations scaled down in size but emphasizing comfortable long-term use of library materials or computers.

Output measures for this role will include circulation, in-library use, and program attendance.

Children's first library experience often occurs when they visit a library with their parents, or a parent, usually several years before they are ready to begin school. This first childhood experience with books, materials, and librarians can determine a lifetime pattern of library use. Story hour may be the first group experience for the preschool child.

It is important that this first experience should express the joy, freedom, and individual interest-tailoring role of the public library rather than the structured learning, study, and curriculum support experience of the school. Of course, the library also provides a learning experience, but it is not a required one. A child who wishes to learn will be encouraged, but need not feel that is the only reason to go to a library.

A Friendly Place

The appearance of the children's room makes the initial impact.

- The space should be inviting and friendly, colorful and approachable.
- The child should feel free to make choices on his or her own.

The child's experience is also marked by what the room feels like.

- Is it welcoming? Are the staff friendly and helpful, but not too pushy?
- Is it comfortable?
- Is it fun?

Essentially, children should feel that the room is for them. This can be achieved by the planner's understanding of the ways children react to environments, recognizing that children make noise and it's OK, and recognizing that children need supervision but not control. With these facts understood, planners can ensure a positive, functioning design.

Flexibility

- Space should lend itself to change and adaptation by the user.
- The child can decide whether to be active or passive in the environment.
- Arrangements should be flexible, consisting of easily movable furniture.
- Stacks, tables, and chairs in a variety of sizes rather than labeling, are used to differentiate the functions of areas.

Variety

A variety of possible spaces and styles of furnishings should be available for programs.

- Work tables and materials should allow children to draw pictures or make puppets as a follow-through for story hour.
- A centralized area for media may be a good idea, as long as it is informal.
- There should be a quiet place available for the child who goes to the library to be quiet and alone.
- Items should be scaled to the child, including coat racks and water fountains.
- Requirements of the handicapped child should be considered. Exceptional children, those who are gifted as well as those who need special encouragement and assistance from the staff, must be equally well served.
- In planning an area for preschoolers, seating for parents should be included so they can comfortably join their children.

Facilities

To encourage children to *enjoy* libraries and be *active* in libraries, they must feel that they can affect the space and its contents. They should be able to create their own study area, select their own materials, and operate their own machines. Essentially, we want to create a space with objects so that children can make it their own. How can we help children do this?

Size and Scale. Think of children as special people. Walk around on your knees to begin to understand how a library looks and operates for people that size. To a four-year old, a five-foot bookstack can be a barrier and 30-inch-high table is more like a ceiling than a working surface.

Private Places. A children's library should contain small alcoves surrounded by low shelves controllable by the staff but accessible to children, so they can pick out a book or game and settle individually or in small groups to enjoy it. Opportunities for children to share experiences with one another as well as to work comfortably alone should alternate in the children's area.

Changing Places. The ability to alter their environment is a deep-seated need in children. Movable objects on wheels, book bins, easels, book trucks, large toy locomotives, and carts can help satisfy this creative urge. Large carpeted boxes 16-inches-high on casters can be pushed together to form a low partition, stage, or protected fort. A panel and dowel system with 2-by-2-foot panels and half-inch dowels can make up a small room. In all of these objects corners must be rounded and material free of splinters and built to withstand heavy punishment.

Friendly Objects. The orderly, tightly shelved, and nearly arranged bookstacks may be quite an inhibiting experience to children. A long counter 26 inches high with a variety of books, games, toys, and machines available to teach, feel, handle, and take out would be a much more inviting experience, especially if combined with glare-free task lighting on the objects.

First Impressions. The first visit of a child to a library can produce impressions that may never be changed. Ideally, this first impression should be of a magical, colorful world of variety, activity, and things to see, hear, and think about offering creative freedom to each child's individuality. The areas should be open and light, full of colorful shapes, spaces, and places. It is to be hoped that this first visit will take place before the child can read, so the room should feature strong visual experiences, some familiar and some totally new and exotic.

Picture Books. They should be arranged in low browsing bins, like phonograph records, with their colorful covers available for easy use.

Video Cassette Players. They should be available so children can view films or see story hours videotaped at the library.

Audio Cassette Players. This equipment enables children to hear stories.

Play-learning Areas. Part of the children's room should be available for open play. A community service resource such as a library is, in a sense, a buying cooperative. Toys and games that an individual could not afford can be purchased for the use of all in the community from the pooling of tax funds. The librarian can serve as the expert in guiding the selection of these materials so that they are durable, safe, and educational, but it is equally important that they be enjoyable experiences for children. One of the virtues of a public library is that children do not have to go to it—they must want to go because it is useful and pleasurable. Large, sturdy wooden toys and other realia are attractive and help in the learning of motor skills and how things work. They should be large enough to sit on and move around. Some libraries lend toys to children. Large shapes—plastic or wooden-that children can pile together or pull apart are often interesting. Immense Tinker Toys or doll houses are also delightful and unique experiences for many children.

Activity Areas. A library can engage the individual in an activity as well as in reading a book or viewing a film. This concept can be a structured program which operates craft, art, and educational activities for groups of preschoolers each day, but even the smallest library can provide story hours once a week. Story hours that combine stories with splendid music and story hours enhanced by puppetry are becoming multisensory appreciation and development experiences in many libraries throughout the country.

In addition to art and craft activities, some libraries encourage poetry and short story writing by posting poems on display walls or publishing them in an annual.

Activity areas for crafts require several 28-inches-high counters made of sturdy butcher-block wood or formica anchored to the floor; a sink and, if possible, a floor with a drain in it for easy cleaning; several lockable cabinets with adjustable shelves inside; walls with burlap-covered homosote for tackboard, and adjustable shelf standards spaced every 30 inches for display of craft work. Avoid carpeting in this area.

Lighting should be fluorescent with sunlight-spectrum lamps and 3/4-inch egg crate parawedge louvers over the work counters, and there should be light tracks or cove lighting for the walls. The lamps should be as invisible as possible to emphasize materials and activities.

Reference and Study Areas and Bookstacks. The transition from children's to adult libraries should be considered carefully in the design of children's areas. Older children requiring study assistance after school and on weekends should have an easily identified *quiet* area where the activity, noise, and bustle will not disturb them. This area should closely resemble the adult library and might even be located near the adult reading room. Children should be freely encouraged to use both adult and children's reference resources.

Chairs. Children's chairs should either be adjustable or available in two or three sizes. Young patrons should be able to shape bean bag chairs to conform to their own bodies. Reclining foam pad pillow combinations, sometimes called pollywogs, should be available on the floor. Simple square or round fabric-covered foam or Ensolite cushions 3 inches thick make admirable work seats.

Work Surfaces. Vertical drawing pads of newsprint and magic markers attached to adjustable height easels with wide, stable feet make admirable surfaces for drawings, notices, and poems. Blackboards can also be mounted on these easels.

Display areas are essential to show children's work, posters, book covers, and topical displays. Wall-mounted bookshelves allow ample room to install homosote above them. This material costs a fraction as much as cork but it is unstable and the surface will crumble, so it should be covered with fabric that can be easily renewed. Cork in a dense rather than a flaky format will, unlike homosote, contract to close tack holes, but it is much more expensive.

Flat horizontal work surfaces such as rectangular tables should be adjustable in height for standing and sitting work as well as for different sizes of children—20 to 30 inches would be a useful range. The surfaces should be nonreflective, and very dark surfaces should be avoided to prevent contrast. Vertical dividers between adjacent spaces, making tables into carrels, are useful in long-term study areas. Individual or criss-cross study carrels are often popular with older children. Six-to nine-inch sides provide sufficient privacy while allowing useful control and avoiding breaking a room up into smaller rooms.

Bookstacks. Forty-six-inch-high children's bookstacks have good book capacity and can be arranged in an alcove system to provide many private areas. Full 90-inch-high adult bookstacks in the children's room have the disadvantage of creating forbidding canyons that children may be reluctant to enter. However, directional stack lighting using angled parawedge louvers will help to create a fascinating pathway between brightly lit books, and step stools at intervals will make the higher shelves easily accessible. The two top shelves can be converted to useful locked storage space, and the cost of this stack will be almost identical to

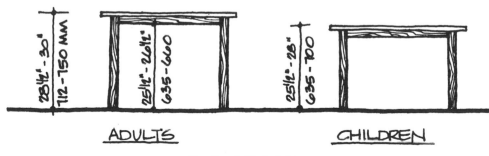

Reading table heights.

a 5-foot stack, which has the disadvantage of reduced storage and a less effective lighting system.

Reference books should be stored on lower 30-inch shelving with the top available for resting books and looking up answers.

Children seem to prefer group tables to study carrels. Work surfaces and chairs should be sized for children.

A Sample Program

Felix Drury, a New Haven architect, has written about the psychology of designing for children. His designs in library children's areas and at day care centers are real breakthroughs in complete children's environments—a marked contrast to the usual scaled-down versions of adult libraries seen in most children's area designs. Following is a sample program for a children's area in a small library:

> The children's area provides space for a full range of services for children of preschool age through the age of twelve and their parent(s). The design and appearance of the children's room will make a lasting impression upon children and parents. The area should express warmth and friendliness and be the place to come to satisfy information and recreational needs.

> Within the children's area are four sections: a preschool area, intermediate area, program area, and librarian's office-workroom. The preschool and intermediate areas are included in one open space, the program area is enclosed, and the librarian's workroom is located off the main area. A service center is located in the intermediate area.

> The preschool area furnishings are colorful and cheerful. Deep browsing bins house picture books for this age level. A combination of colored cushions and play chairs accommodate the children, and lounge chairs are available for parents to read with their children. Puzzles and other toys are also available. This area will be noisy, and some special considerations should be made to absorb and isolate sound.

> The intermediate area houses the main children's fiction and nonfiction collection. Shelving is steel, 60 inches high and 10 inches deep, with backstops to accommodate all sizes of children's books. Reference shelving is 12 inches deep and 30 inches high with tops available for resting books and looking up answers. Paperbacks are on display in rotating racks. Seating consists of tables and chairs, a grouping of carrels, and lounge chairs for relaxing or studying.

> The activity area is a separate area with drapes covering the windows. It is used for story hour, library orientations, children's films, and special pro-

grams. This area will have sound absorbent features and a projection screen. The flooring in the room should be sound absorbent and stain-resistant carpet.

The children's service center is an information center. At the service desk there is seating for one staff member and two children for consultation. The same counter also accommodates a CRT terminal. Staff members have visual control of the entire children's area from this station.

The workroom provides a desk, as much counter work space (37 inches high) as possible, and ample storage of supplies. The children's librarian's office has a view of the service center.

Pegs for coats are provided in the children's area. The entire area is carpeted with durable, stain-resistant material.

YOUNG ADULT AREA

The primary purpose of the young adult area is to serve the recreational and personal development needs of adolescents. Their informational needs will be met primarily from the adult nonfiction and general reference collections. The young adult area for youth up to eighteen years of age, still in school or not, serves as a bridge between the children's room and the adult areas.

The young adult area should reassure young adults that the library is indeed there for them. Their special needs are for information to complete school projects, pursue hobbies, seek self-help information, and find materials and programs that meet their recreational requirements.

The young adult area should provide teenagers with a place where they can relax and chat with friends. It should provide an attractive space for adolescents where they will feel welcome, not be judged or graded or subjected to criticism from adult users. They will use this area to browse through recreational fiction, records, and tapes. There should be a listening center where an individual can listen to music without disturbing others. There will be magazines, career guides, and brochures and books relating to adolescent health and other personal concerns. Young adults should be able to talk with friends or type a term paper.

There should be comfortable seating, including lounge chairs for relaxing or reading. There should be a typewriter table, typewriter, and chair for doing reports, as well as wall space for posters and a bulletin board for library program notices and other items of interest to young people. The room should have sound absorbent features, as the noise level is apt to be higher than elsewhere in the library.

COMMUNITY ACTIVITIES CENTER ROLE

The library is a center for community cultural events—art shows, programs, films, lectures, and meeting of many community organizations. Output measures include program attendance.

Meeting Facilities

There should be an auditorium sized large enough to support major cultural events such as orchestra performances, ballet or dance, and country music. Considerations in selecting an appropriate size include:

- Other town facilities
- Nearby regional facilities
- Potential audience
- Revenue potential
- Library staff capabilities

Design considerations include:

- Acoustics (live for music, absorbent for film)
- Fixed or movable seating (clear sight lines verses flexibility)
- Storage for chairs and tables
- Food and beverage service potential
- Piano delivery and storage (wide clearance doors)
- Separate, controllable entrance
- Restroom and coat room facilities
- Arrival and departure of large groups as opposed to the usual small group or individual arrival pattern.
- Seat and aisle spacing
- Audio-visual equipment storage
- Green room for performers to change or rest
- Projection—video, front or rear projection, sound isolation

Small meeting facilities for groups of ten to fifty people will be needed for group discussion or literacy tutorials as well as small meetings.

Multipurpose Room

A multipurpose meeting and program room should be designed to help fulfill the objectives of the library as a cultural center and community meeting place. First priority is given to its use for library-sponsored programs and, secondly, for community public meetings. They may be reserved for private use only when not needed for the first two priorities.

The multipurpose room must be equipped with a public address system, film speakers, microphones, stackable chairs, adjustable folding tables that can be stored out of sight, display capabilities, lectern, and projection screen. A separate projection room and kitchen serves this area. The acoustics should be designed with priorities in the following order.

1. lectures and meetings
2. film or video viewing
3. musical performances
4. dramatic performances

The meeting room should be accessible from the main library but should have also an entrance and exit directly to the street for after-hours use. Sound and light should be capable of being darkened in daylight hours, and walls should be designed for the display of art. It should have neutral colors and lighting on tracks 3 feet out from walls.

There should be a 70-inch-wide door between the delivery entrance and the multipurpose room to accommodate bringing a piano in and out.

INDEPENDENT LEARNING CENTER ROLE

The independent learning center role of the public library affects building planning for three reasons:

- Materials to support a variety of independent learning objectives require a somewhat larger book collection.
- Quiet study areas for long-term use will be in greater demand.
- Staff consultations to assist users in satisfying independent learning objectives will require user seating at the information center.

These considerations will affect building size in relation to its intensity of use. In many public libraries support of the independent learning role may be a low-priority matter, supplied as an informal activity requiring little additional space but not emphasized or promoted.

THE FORMAL SUPPORT TO EDUCATION ROLE

This role requires libraries to become knowledgeable about educational opportunities in the community. This may affect building planning by increasing the depth of subject strengths to support term paper research, especially in the areas of periodical indexes and back issues. Recently this has come to mean careful planning for work stations to access CD-ROM indexes and full-text microfilm, fiche readers, and printers, and remote data-base online searching.

Staff-patron coordination for these functions may have considerable impact on information center size and on work stations close to the information center. Larger libraries may consider high-density compact stacks for housing back issue periodicals.

Long-term study needs may also be affected in libraries with strong formal support for education objectives. These libraries will need additional user study areas and work stations.

Group study assignments and mass use of materials by large groups of students are often extraordinarily difficult, since public libraries are designed basically for individual use. Close coordination with school librarians and teachers may lessen the negative impacts of these assignments and provide more effective help for students' curriculum-related needs. This responsibility may be more that of the school media center, but a continued, evident need for a public library response may result in the design of a public library homework center with multiple copies of books and articles and group study facilities and nearby work stations.

Remote or distance learning systems may be closely related to this formal support role and will also need special communication facilities, including video reception and production.

LIBRARY PROFILE

In summary, this new planning process might result in these differences in a building program:

Roles	Output Measures
Community activities center	Program attendance per capita
Community information center	Reference questions per capita
Formal education support center	In-library materials use per capita
Independent learning center	In-library materials use per capita

Roles	Output Measures
Community activities center	Program attendance per capita
Community information center	Reference questions per capita
Formal education support center	In-library materials use per capita
Independent learning center	In-library materials use per capita
Popular materials library	Circulation per capita
Preschooler's door to learning	Circulation per capita
Reference library	Reference questions per capita
Research center	Reference completion rate (percentage of questions answered correctly)

A Comparison of Book and Study Libraries Serving the Same Population

A library (*book library*) serving a 20,000 population and role priorities as follows:

Popular materials	40%
Reference	20%
Preschoolers	20%
Community activities	20%

might have an outline building program such as:

Book capacity	100,000	10,000 square feet
Seating	100	3,000 square feet
Program seating	100	1,200 square feet

Another library (*study library*) with role priorities such as:

Popular materials	30%
Reference	50%
Preschoolers	10%
Community activities	10%

might have an outline building program such as:

Book capacity	60,000	6,000 square feet
Seating	150	4,500 square feet
Program seating	50	600 square feet

This is depicted in the comparative diagram on the following page.

Comparative Diagram of
Book and Study Libraries Building Program

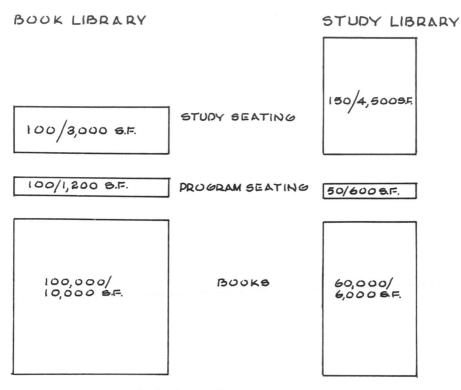

BOOK LIBRARY   STUDY LIBRARY

STUDY SEATING

100/3,000 S.F.   150/4,500 S.F.

100/1,200 S.F.   PROGRAM SEATING   50/600 S.F.

100,000/   BOOKS   60,000/
10,000 S.F.   6,000 S.F.

Both Libraries Serve 20,000 People.

6

Library Functions Related to Library Roles

BOOKSTACKS

As libraries grow in size, it becomes increasingly confusing to break up the bookstacks into irregular configurations. In using both the Dewey and Library of Congress book classification systems, the reader will find it easier to use bookstacks with a continuous sequential numbering system without breaks for seating. For several reasons, it is also most economical to design a building with all the bookstacks in one continuous pattern.

The larger the library the greater the necessity to maintain a single consecutively numbered bookstack for easy convenience in finding a book. People will spend the least amount of time in the bookstack, so consistent temperature is less important here than elsewhere. However, the need to read call numbers and spine titles on the lower shelves requires careful attention to lighting fixture reflectors and louvres and mandates light-colored floor surfaces and shelves to get light on the bottom-shelf books. Graphic systems on end panels and shelves that clearly indicate book sequencing, such as Dewey Break labels, will greatly help users.

Load-bearing capabilities of 150 pounds per square foot live load for conventional shelving 90 inches high, and 300 pounds per square foot for high-density compact stacks, require an unusually strong structural system. Top bracing structurally attached to the building and a stack aisle of 40 inches also set this pattern of highly formalized space in contrast to less structured readers' seating.

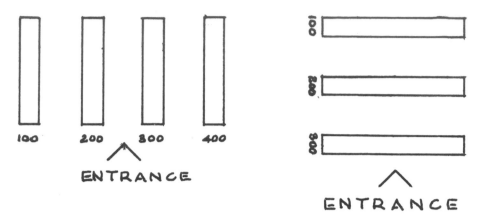

To orient users trying to find a particular book quickly and easily, stack-end panels and aisles should be immediately visible and clearly marked for access from the first entrance into the building.

Bookstack size projections need to include these considerations:

- Present number of books shelved
- Present circulation-seasonal fluctuations in books needing to be shelved
- Present configuration—aisle widths, stack height
- Book acquisitions—mix of fiction, nonfiction, reference, and over-sized books
- Oversized book shelving procedures—integrated, bottom or middle shelf, or separate section
- Future networking capabilities and potentials
- Percentage of withdrawal—net annual additions
- Frequency of use objective—How many rarely used books will the library retain? For example, 10 percent to 20 percent that have *not* been borrowed in the past three years?
- Gifts—cash and in kind
- Multiple copy selection and withdrawal procedures
- Promotional activities
- Population projections for areas from which library users are most likely to come
- Educational demographic changes, especially in the immediate neighborhood

- Parking access
- Pedestrian access
- Nearby library resources and user access to these resources
- Desire of the community to support a large library

Stack aisles must be visible from the staff area for supervision. A bookstack area should have graphic signs and integrated lighting for convenient access. For convenience in finding a particular book as well as for good staff control, the book collection should be placed in a continuous sequential one-pattern bookstack area. Books are consecutively numbered, and any break in the shelving pattern will confuse the user. Bookstack design should also include these considerations:

- A standard section of bookstacks is three feet long and 84 to 90 inches high.
- A double-faced section will have an eventual maximum capacity of three hundred volumes if all seven shelves on each side are used with space left for shelving returns.
- Stacks must be braced across the top and attached to the building structure to prevent collapse.
- A range of shelving should be a maximum of six sections long to make it possible for readers to move easily from one aisle to the next. Each 18-foot double-faced, six-section range will hold 1,800 books.
- Ranges should be spaced 60 inches apart on centers, leaving an aisle 44 inches wide if 8-inch shelving is installed.
- Fluorescent lights shielded by angled parawedge louvers mounted about three inches above the top of the stacks provides optimum lighting with minimum glare. They can be suspended from ceiling.
- Seating should not be combined with stacks because this would require a wider aisle and larger, less efficient area. Carrels can be across from the end of the stack.
- Gliding step stools should be kept in each aisle to facilitate reaching the top shelves.
- Bookstacks require a floor load-bearing capacity of 150 pounds per square foot.
- Art and oversized books will require shelving 12-inches-deep.
- Bookstops should be provided to prevent books from being pushed back off the shelves. Non-removable thick book supports should be provided for each shelf.

Aisle Space In Busy Stacks.

- Canopies are unnecessary and often create light shadows from overhead lighting.
- Determining bookstack capacity accurately can be accomplished using these average running foot capacities: adult books-nine per foot, reference books-seven per foot, bound periodicals-seven per foot, and children's books-fifteen per foot but often placed in lower stacks 60 inches or five shelves high.

Book locators such as Dewey break locators should be placed at the beginning of each major decimal section: 100, 110, 120, etc., visible down the aisle to aid the user in finding a book quickly.

Compact Stack Area—High Density

Stacks on tracks, which will be accessible to staff only, provide compact storage. These stacks can easily be moved by hand while preserving the safety of users. These require a floor capable of supporting 300 pounds per square foot compared to the 150 pounds per square foot floor load of regular bookstacks. Therefore, these should be installed at grade level. They hold up to forty-five books per square foot.

This area can be used to store back issues of periodicals. Holiday books and other infrequently used materials can also be shelved here.

Safety Features

- Floor pressure device immobilizing stacks when pressure is applied
- Obstruction pressure sensors on shelf edge and bottom shelf
- Motion detectors at stack access points
- Closing resistance clutch slippage device.

Compact High Density Stack Performance Considerations

- Track structural rigidity for floor unevenness
- Stack bracing across the top
- Rail shape and steel quality for resistance to deformation
- Ease of starting and stopping
- Force necessary to continue motion
- Maintenance—location, response time, track record, and back-up
- Lighting—pantograph suspension system and automatic switch-off
- Flanged wheels or other device to prevent derailing
- Interfaces—fire prevention (Halon), security, building security
- Manual operation if power fails—convenience required
- Track height and floor system

Other Considerations

- Installation experience of vendors
- Complexity of purchase and installation responsibility—single source
- Annual maintenance cost
- Open aisle width
- Warranties
- Motor for each range?
- Are gears positively connected to turning controls, slippage?
- Number of installations
- Nationality of vendor and manufacturer (in case of state bid requirement)
- Advantages: less cost for building, less cost for utilities, operating retention of larger collection of lesser-used materials, and in-house availability
- Disadvantages: potential of accidents to public and staff (insurance

risk); easy, open, confidential access denied if designated staff only; additional staff time needed, cost and maintenance of equipment, load-bearing capacity of floor requires 300 pounds per square foot capacity, and removes materials from numbered sequence, making users look two places for each book.

Although this alternative has disadvantages some part of the library should be constructed so that this alternative can be a future option for storage of little-used materials.

STAFF WORK AREA DESIGN CONSIDERATIONS

Efficiency

Staff technical service work areas must help efficiency, which is expressed in the detailed yet flexible design of public service areas. In order to accomplish work with least effort the circulation service area must incorporate these functions:

Circulation Center

- *Check-out* must be convenient to exit because of theft detection sensors; it should be wired for computer wands and lasers, have a 36- to 40-inch high public surface, a 30-inch staff work surface, and an interchangeable space below surface for mobile files, drawers, shelves, form slots, computer printers, telephones, and modems.
- *Check-in* must have dual-level public and staff surfaces and self-service return slot with mobile depressible return cart.
- *Reserve* (storage and pick up).
- *Computer* having wiring with nearby circuit breakers for easy electrical maintenance.
- *Self-service* with electronic theft detection related to check-out function.

Reference Center (stand up and seated public service locations)

- *Ready reference* books
- *Terminals* for staff and public
- *Stand-up* index reference
- *Modular* mobile files and stands
- *FAX-telephone* stations for staff and public
- *Lighting* (task and color corrected)

Effectiveness

Effectiveness of staff is directly related to staff perceptions of the work environment and how they feel about the aesthetics of where they work. These perceptions may be greatly affected by sunlight, temperature, humidity, and light control. In staff work areas used for long periods of time these perceptions become increasingly important. Staff members working for four hours in the same spot require more thoughtful design solutions than users coming to the library for five minutes for a book to read. Staff work areas should have sunlight, green plants, staff-controlled temperature and lighting, long-distance views for eye relief, and personalized work stations with easy adjustability of chairs and work surfaces and a choice of furnishings, equipment, and decorative accessories.

Library employees perform a wide variety of tasks during a busy work day. Depending on their specialty and the demands of the moment, a great deal of time is spent at a work station using a computer keyboard, working with library materials, or consulting with library users and co-workers. Two issues should be addressed in the design of work stations:

1. Comfort. The seating, work surfaces, and other furnishings must be comfortable and provide good support, especially to the sacro-lumbar area, for staff members who must sit at the work stations for long periods of time.
2. Adjustability. All aspects of the work station should be adjustable. This flexibility is critical for a number of reasons:

   - Workers themselves vary greatly in height, weight, and body proportions.
   - Jobs differ. One worker may spend seven or eight hours a day at a keyboard working on a report, while another employee spends the same time consulting on the telephone about a new library program. The following day the roles could be reversed.
   - Equipment and technology will certainly change. A work station designed for today's computer system may become irrelevant when the technology changes tomorrow.
   - Several people may use the same work station. Libraries are frequently open eighty or more hours per week and the staff often works in shifts. A work station designed for a 240-pound reference librarian six-foot, four-inches tall, will not be appropriate for one who stands 5 feet and weighs 100 pounds.

Seating

The user should be able to adjust the height of the seat and its back rest. Furthermore, the back rest and seat pan should be laterally adjustable so that the user can move the back rest fore and aft and change the seat deflection from flat to a somewhat backward angle. All adjustment levers must be readily accessible and easy to use, staff members should not have to get on their knees or turn chairs upside down to make adjustments. Arm rests should be adjustable and removable. The chair itself should move and swivel to allow the worker to perform a wide range of activities.

Desks and Work Surfaces

Ideally, library workers should have desks and work surfaces that can be adjusted from 22 to 45 inches from the floor. Normal desk height is 26 to 28 inches. The higher work surface permits workers with back injuries to use a keyboard or library materials while standing. At minimum, the work area must include an adjustable keyboard pan that enables a sitting worker to maintain the upper and lower arms at a 90-degree angle (upper arm vertical, forearm horizontal) and the wrists 10 to 20 degrees from horizontal. A tilting keyboard pan would also help improve the wrist angle. The ideal work area is 60 inches wide but should be at least 30 inches wide to permit opening books or using documents or other media. Leg clearance should be at least 24 inches wide and 16 inches deep.

Computer Equipment

The library's role in the Information Age demands increased reliance on computers and related technology. Librarians create, maintain, and search a host of local and remote databases; they use word processing equipment to write reports, letters, and other documents; they use spreadsheets and other productivity software to plan budgets and manage the organization.

Local Area Networks and connectivity are important aspects of a library's use of this technology. Design features must reflect the need to power and connect equipment in each work station as well as between the different departments. J-channels, ramps, grommeted openings for bundled cables, and power poles are important design features. The work station needs room for a variety of hardware, including printers, paper supplies, and storage devices like hard disks and CD-ROM disc systems. Shelving for manuals and supporting documents is also important.

Screens

Placement of the CRT or VDT screen is also a primary concern. The screen should be approximately 18 inches from the worker's eyes and as low as possible, ideally recessed into the desk surface itself. The screen should never be above normal eye level. In the best situation, the user will be able to raise, lower, tilt, and swivel the screen to suit individual physical requirements.

Visual fatigue can be minimized by correct lighting. Artificial or natural light that is too bright can cause glare of a wash-out effect. VDT should not be placed next to windows, but, when this is necessary, the screen should be at a right angle to the plane of the window. Polarized glare screens may be helpful while blinds can also control reflected glare.

On the other hand, dim lighting can cause the operator to strain to read the screen or paper documents on the desk. What is adequate lighting during the day may be completely inappropriate in the evening. Because proper lighting is a relative concept, adjustability in task lighting at the work station is important. Workers are more productive when they can adjust the intensity and the angle of light in their work area.

TECHNICAL PROCESSES

Purpose and Function

Technical processes house the functions behind the scenes necessary to successful and efficient public service. Materials are ordered, received, cataloged, and processed. Other functions include binding, mending, and serials check-in.

Most work will take place in a large, central work area with several functional subareas. There will be architecturally separate areas for a director's office, new book area, and utility room.

Staff and Working Hours

The technical processes department has a permanent staff, but staff from other departments in the library will consult from time to time with department staff and use their facilities and materials, such as publisher's catalogs. The peak period of work activity will be 9:00 to 5:00 PM, Monday through Friday.

General Conditions

The arrangement of work spaces, location of equipment and, most important in the design stage, color scheme and lighting should promote productivity and attention to detail over relatively long periods of time. Space for individual expression, such as areas for green plants and wall space for posters and decorations, is necessary where work is unrelieved by the variety and the immediate satisfaction of public contact. Cork bulletin boards should be placed at work stations so that staff members can easily refer to schedules, procedural memos and other temporary notes. At work stations a 2-by-3-foot board is sufficient, with 4-by-6-foot board near the office and shipping areas.

Natural lighting from windows should be augmented by task-oriented lighting from lamps and fixtures. These should have flexible switching patterns.

Climate control is essential for staff members who spend long hours at work stations. In so far as possible, staff should be able to control the climate.

Proximity and Traffic

Location of the department is also important to efficient operation. The area should be close to other library departments yet acoustically and visually separate. Traffic from other departments or to frequently used areas in the technical processes department should not be routed through work areas.

Main Work Area

Design features should allow for additional computer systems, including computer cabling facilities to link computer work stations through a local area network. At some future date, all desks may have computer work stations tied into the network and to work stations in other departments.

The followiing functional area sizes and relationships differ widely dependent on size of library and internal operational considerations:

The order department is where materials-books, video cassettes, recordings, and so forth first arrive in the library. The shipping boxes are opened and their contents inventoried here. Materials are then routed to the appropriate departments or branches of the library. Acquisition records for original and duplicate materials are also maintained and processed here. The area will have long counters along a wall for receiving, shipping, and distributing materials.

The book order room is an architecturally separate area where librarians from the branches and other departments will examine new books and recommend purchase of additional copies of those items. Most nonfiction books will go directly to this area after receipt by the order department. The book order room should be sited to minimize outside traffic through technical processes department work areas.

The cataloging department is where the materials are cataloged and classified. This area requires space for book trucks with materials to be processed.

The physical processing area is where books and other materials are prepared for use by the public. This area will have counter space and work tables for pasting book pockets and applying labels and space for book trucks.

The area will have built-in counters with storage underneath and shelving above. This area should be located near elevators and major traffic areas to minimize disruptions from outside staff using catalogs in the area. Carrels or desk shelving should be nearby to facilitate catalog use. A sink with hot and cold faucets will be located in this area.

7

Special Considerations: Graphics, Lighting, and Energy

GRAPHICS

- In selecting size, consider background and distance.
- Consider how the sign will be lighted as compared to its background.
- Use a simple, direct, familiar, easily obtainable type style, such as Helvetica.
- Graphics can be architecturally and aesthetically pleasing as well as functional.
- Location, colors, furnishings, and lighting can be as useful in affecting behavior as graphics. All should be coordinated.
- Avoid negative signs, especially large permanent ones.
- Signs are seldom permanently usable; consider ease of replacement.
- Flyers, posters, maps, and directories may be more appropriate than signs.
- Plan graphics early in design development as part of the library's function, not after a building is completed.
- Standard height-centerpoint 60 inches.
- Use capitals and lower case rather than all upper case.
- Never stack letters, as

                           B
                           O
                           O
                           K
                           S

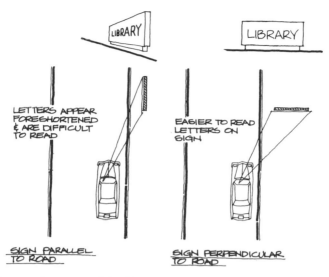

Proper placement of the library sign is essential to its effectiveness.

- Arrow panels used to indicate directions should always be produced separately from letter panels so that different letter panels can be substituted.
- A sign schedule, order and specifications, should be sent out four months before a new library building is to be occupied.
- User categories should be identified and their typical destinations charted before sign specifications are prepared. Plan by: a) user category; b) user destination, c) plot traffic flow; d) decision points; e) message.
- Sign size should be 1 inch high for every 50 feet of visibility so that a 2-inch-high sign can be seen from 100 feet away.
- A dark background with light letters is easier to read than the other way around because there is less glare.

LIGHTING

Lighting has an exceedingly important part to play not only in the design but in the function of libraries. The way in which people use the library and their feelings about the building are often determined by making the proper choice in lighting design. Lighting will not only make the building easy to use but will affect behavior and give people a comfortable feeling about the library.

How the Eye Works. The human eye has a mechanism for regulating the amount of light that comes into it, allowing less light into the eye as the amount of light increases. For this reason, increasing the amount of light in a space will not necessarily make it easier for the eye to see. Standards indicating the amount of footcandles necessary for general illumination are not always a satisfactory measure of the ability to see effectively in the library. Most lighting consultants today feel that the amount of light required in libraries and classrooms ten years ago was excessive and actually contributed to poor visibility of library materials.

There is also an effect of color on the muscles of the eye. These muscles work hardest to accommodate to red color while green color is the most relaxing. This was the reason for the type of institutional green found in many government buildings in the forties and fifties. There has been a recent flurry of interest in the effect of color on behavior. It has been determined, for example, that proper color and lighting could reduce the extent of violence in prison environments.

Understanding how the eye works and how the operation of the eye affects human behavior is an important consideration in the design of libraries. Library planners and architects should determine the types of behavior desired in various parts of the library.

Natural light is by far the best way to light a library but natural light in this sense does not mean direct light from the sun. Design the library so that direct sunlight never strikes a book or a place where a reader might be sitting. Direct sunlight will preclude any possibility of cooling that location, and the light will be so bright that it will be almost impossible to see anything. It is important that the building overhangs and that the way in which the building is sited prevent direct sunlight from ever striking a reader location.

Indirect sunlight coming through windows, skylights or clerestories will provide the most pleasing and easy-to-see light. The natural lighting locations may create problems for heating in the winter time and cooling in the summer, so heating and ventilating systems must be carefully articulated to window design. Windows and even clerestories cannot properly illuminate all parts of the building; since libraries operate for almost a third of the working day after sundown in the late fall and winter, it is important not to depend too much on natural light for any building location.

Bright Lights. Natural light from the sun, not exactly overhead but coming through a skylight or through a window, can be as bright as 1,000 footcandles. People who are partially sighted find that they can read much more easily with this intense natural light as long as it is indirect. The reason is a phenomena called 'inter reflection'. That is, if the light strikes the reading surface from a variety of angles, the effect is to eliminate glare and to provide the best possible lighting. This corresponds to indirect lighting from a dome ceiling.

Frank Lloyd Wright, in his design for the Marin County Courthouse, north of San Francisco, tried to produce such a reading room in the library. When I visited the Marin County Library I was appalled at the low level of lighting in this area, but after spending a few minutes in the library I realized that there were a lot of older people with glasses in the center of the room reading happily in what seemed to be totally inadequate lighting conditions. Wright had designed the room with a pale-colored dome similar to the sphere dome design set up in lighting laboratories to test lighting effectiveness. He then placed lights at the base of this dome reflecting upward but concealed from the direct line of sight of users. The result was a low amount of footcandles on the reading surfaces (lower than thirty-footcandles), sufficient light to read by since it struck the reading surface from a wide variety of angles, eliminating glare and producing a very useful kind of light. In one recently designed library addition, an effort was made to produce this type of inter-reflective, indirect light by shining high intensity fixtures onto a high ceiling for indirect light throughout the room; in Portland, Maine, high intensity discharge indirect light is used in two-foot square fixtures in a low ceiling.

Artificial Light that stimulates the effect of indirect sunlight is by far the most effective light for a library but is very difficult to achieve. Large amounts of energy are required to provide sufficient indirect light bounced off the ceiling of a library reading room to come anywhere near the amount of indirect light generated from the sun. In buildings where this has been tried, the lighting levels are much lower than that of indirect sunlight, and for older people this may be a problem. Light that comes directly onto a book from an artificial light source usually lacks the inter-reflection (light striking from a wide variety of angles) that prevents glare. Artificial direct light usually has a high component of glare which can be minimized by a proper selection of covers. There are two kinds of lenses and louvers. Lenses cover the light source completely and are usually designed so they have a particular effect on that light source. An acrylic prism lens spreads light from fluorescent fixtures so that fixtures can be spaced far apart. This can often result in economy of operation but it does not eliminate glare. Opal lenses diffusing light from fluorescent fixtures will not spread light as effectively, but glare will be reduced at some cost to light output. In this type of installation more fixtures will be necessary but there will be less annoying glare.

In some instances louvers are preferable to lenses. The louver allows the light to come through directly. There are two types of louvers. The egg crate louver is simply a grid of squares allowing the light to pass through but preventing glare when viewed at an angle. The parabolic wedge louver diffuses light even more than the egg crate, and in a fairly low ceiling installation, the parawedge makes the light fixture seem almost dark. However, the parawedge is very directional, preventing the light from spreading underneath the fixture; therefore more fixtures may be necessary. An interesting effect of the parawedge louver is that a person reading for a long period of time is not annoyed by a bright ceiling distracting from concentration. Parawedge louvers also have the advantage of providing an interesting variation in light and dark areas in a room.

Track lighting, recently popular in office buildings and libraries, directs light on use areas, thus reducing light in other areas, reducing energy consumption, and providing for an interesting and varied type of lighting. However, this does not conserve energy in large areas of uniform use and limits flexibility.

A type of lighting found in office buildings in the 1950's and '60's was known as a *luminous ceiling,* in which fluorescent tubes were placed in the ceiling and lenses hung beneath them to spread the light as effectively as possible. The effect produced a distribution of light so that a minimum amount of energy would produce a maximum amount of uniform lighting at the reading surface. This resulted in lighting levels as high as 150 candles, and the theory was that this would provide a less tiring lighting solution for people working on a wide variety of fine tasks over a long period of time. However, very little was done with these lenses to reduce glare. Both direct and reflected glare were very annoying especially when combined with a glossy type of coated paper stock. The other difficulty with luminous ceiling installations is that they do not provide any variety of lighting. They were dull, uninteresting spaces characterized by bright, glary ceilings that often motivated people working in those spaces to wish for the 'good ole days' when they could wear visors to prevent the glare from shining into their eyes.

Lighting Sources. There are several types of lighting sources available. Mercury vapor, sodium vapor, and tungsten halogen are all types of high intensity discharge lighting. They produce the maximum amount of lumen output for the minimum amount of electrical consumption and are very efficient lighting in this sense. However, they are point-source lighting and produce a considerable amount of heat, the ballasts are noisy, and they are shiny, bright and glary. They should seldom be used in a library as a direct source. Color is also a problem in high-intensity discharge lighting. Color can vary from a bright yellow of the sodium vapor to a blue-violet light produced in some mercury vapor fixtures. Two colors may be combined in order to provide a balance by the time the light is reflected from the ceiling. It is very important to use bulb guards over high-intensity discharge lighting since, very infrequently, a bulb may burst and the glass could be harmful.

Fluorescent lights work by an electrical current exciting gas in a long thin glass tube. The coating of the tube determines the color of the light which can vary from cool white with a color rating of 4200 degrees Kelvin to warm white fluorescent light with a rating of 3000 degrees Kelvin.

This contrasts with a rating of 2850 Kelvin for incandescent bulbs and 2100 degrees Kelvin for sodium vapor high-intensity discharge lighting. All of this compares with the 5400 degree Kelvin color produced by natural sunlight. When fluorescent bulbs first came out, the cool white fluorescents produced the greatest lumen output. Therefore they were preferred over warm white which, although closer in color to incandescent bulbs and more flattering to human skin color, were much less efficient producing lower lumen output. Improvements in efficiency, however, have cancelled this difference, and warm white fluorescent lamps now produce as many lumens as cool white. Recently introduced cool white deluxe color is a pleasing solution.

Several specialty companies, such as VERILUX, have also experimented to try to find bulbs that match the color of daylight. The VERILUX bulb comes close to the 5400 degree Kelvin color of daylight. Their bulbs are often used in diamond testing and in art departments where color rendition is extremely important. The VERILUX lamp is more expensive than the standard lamp and produces a slightly lower lumen output.

Incandescent light producing 2805 degree Kelvin color rendition is what most of us are used to. They are a point source of light and are relatively inefficient compared to fluorescent or high-intensity discharge lamps. The average incandescent lamp with 100 watts rating will deliver about 800 lumens while a fluorescent lamp burning forty watts may produce as high as 3000 lumens of light. The rated life of most incandescent lamps is less than 1,000 hours while the rated life of a fluorescent lamp can be more than 10,000 hours. The incandescent lamp has to be changed more often and the bulb is almost as expensive as the fluorescent lamp which lasts ten times as long. There have been a few changes which are of interest in incandescent lamps. General Electric is now producing an elliptical reflector bulb in addition to their conventional reflector lamp. The elliptical reflector bulb is more concentrated than the standard reflector bulb. However, both the elliptical reflector and the standard reflector lamp cost about three to four times what a standard 75 or 100 watt lamp will cost. A standard lamp set in an elliptical reflector will produce about the same result.

It is very important when purchasing incandescent lamp fixtures to be certain that they are well ventilated. The ventilation will reduce the heat in the fixture and make the bulb last considerably longer.

Library Functions. Library bookstacks cover the largest single functional area in any library; therefore the selection of lighting for these bookstacks is an important lighting decision. Fluorescent lights are usually the choice in bookstack areas since their long length is much more effective than the point-source lighting produced by high-intensity discharge or incandescent fixtures. Whether the fluorescent lights are placed perpendicular or parallel to the way the stack runs is an important decision. There is no one correct method. The perpendicular type of placement will result in less costly installation and greater flexibility. However, the parallel placement will result in more comfort for the user and improved lighting levels in the stack.

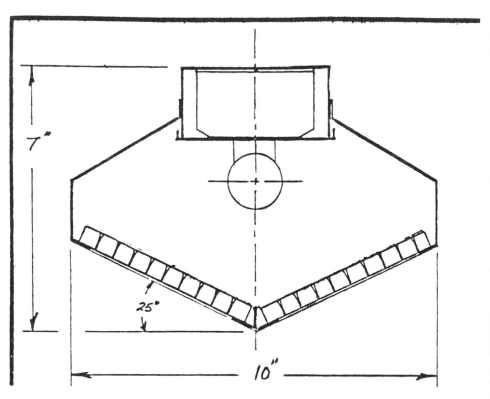

A Bookstack Light Fixture.

In the bookstack area the behavioral pattern of the patron is to stay in the bookstack for a relatively short period of time, therefore during that time the books should be easy to find and the light should be directed onto the books rather than onto the aisle or the head of the searcher. It is dif-

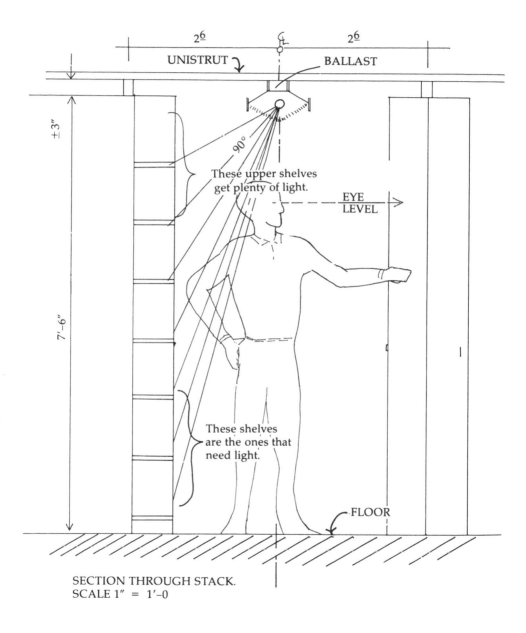

SECTION THROUGH STACK.
SCALE 1″ = 1′–0

Lighting in a Bookstack Aisle.

ficult to find a good solution for bookstack lighting simply because bookstacks are vertical and lighting horizontal. The light has to cover an area from seven feet off the ground down to the floor itself. Ideally, lights should be installed vertically every three feet along the bookstack with shields to prevent the lights from shining in the eye of the library user. To make bookstack areas most flexible, the lighting is often attached to the ceiling itself rather than to the bookstacks. The bookstack arrangement may change; therefore it is less expensive to install the light in the ceiling and change the bookstacks underneath it. Probably the most inexpensive installation is for lights to be installed on a grid perpendicular to the bookstack ranges. The problem with ceiling installation is the variation of light intensity. With a light meter held vertically, there will probably be sixty footcandles on the top shelf near the light source and this will drop to five foot-candles or less on the bottom shelf. Most of the lighting on the bottom shelf will come from reflection from the floor, and if the floor is carpeted as it is in most stack areas, there will be very little reflection and therefore a very low light level. Of course, carpeting the floor is very attractive, comfortable, and quiet but not effective in terms of light reflection.

Carrel lighting or reading table lighting is an important consideration since carrels or desks will be occupied for a much longer time than will bookstacks, and lighting is important for the long term comfort of the user. An article that appeared in *Lighting Design and Application* magazine, November 1971, showed that supplemental lighting mounted to the side instead of in front of the user substantially reduces veiling reflections. Therefore their recommendation was that carrels should be designed with the lighting mounted on the sides rather than in the rear. Of course this is a difficult design problem and a costly one since it requires two lighting fixtures instead of one and since the light fixture has to be strong enough to throw light over the full width of the carrel.

It would be interesting to set up fluorescent lights mounted on the sides of the table or carrel with reflectors that would bounce the light the full distance across the reading surface. An index table in the old University of Texas library building constructed in the early twentieth century used such lighting and is one of the most effective index tables I have ever seen in any library. The fixtures, of course, are incandescent, not fluorescent, but they are beautiful brass tubes set to reflect the light across the full length of the table.

A summary list of lighting considerations includes:

- Select lenses or louvers that diffuse light and prevent glare.

- Locate fixtures to minimize ceiling brightness and veiling reflections caused by light striking the viewing surface at a 45-degree angle (especially difficult with glossy coated paper such as magazines).
- Limit light intensity variation in small rooms or contiguous areas.
- Use low-intensity light in nonreading areas.
- Costs for electricity and maintenance will increase, so install fixtures and lenses that burn cool and are simple to clean and replace.
- Use electronic fluorescent ballasts.
- Use sodium or tungsten halogen for outdoor parking lights.
- Use CAPSYLITE for spotlights.
- Use fluorescent lights for high hats.
- Avoid direct sunlight which is unpredictable and difficult to control. Ultra-violet light damages paper and bindings.
- Avoid glare and reflection by careful selection of diffusers, louvers, and light locations.
- Let users control lighting.
- Parawedge louvers minimize ceiling brightness and veiling reflections, but provide directional lighting and do not eliminate direct glare.
- The bat wing reflector spreads light over a wide area and provides inexpensive, evenly distributed lighting.
- White ceilings and white walls will increase light, especially in small rooms.
- Visibility in a room is affected by size of room, color and contrast within the room, and brightness of lamps.
- Warm white fluorescent lamps (not Deluxe) provide better rendition of skin tones than cool white lamps. Cool white deluxe lamps resemble sunlight.

HVAC: Heating, Ventilating, Air Conditioning

HVAC, or heating, ventilating, and air conditioning, is too important to leave to the experts. Plans for this area will not only affect the comfort of library users but staff productivity and, ultimately, the economic viability of library services.

User Comfort. One of the unusual characteristics of library use is that a small percentage of intensive users spend many hours working passively in one location. During this time the user's metabolism often slows down gradually, lowering body temperature. For this reason, most libraries should have a small area set aside with a constant temperature of 70 degrees Fahrenheit.

At the same time, another obvious library building characteristic is that the building contains a variety of other spaces that have varied HVAC requirement:

Long-term seating	70 degrees
Material storage	55–75 degrees
Staff work area	68 degrees
Supply storage	50–80 degrees

Careful planning for energy conservation makes it possible to locate the storage areas, which require the most space, to act as passive insulators for the long-term and staff use areas, which require most constant temperatures.

Solar Energy

Active solar buildings use the sun's energy to heat or cool a space. A variety of methods of generating electricity, from solar panels to photovoltaic cells, have been proposed for active solar buildings. As fuel costs increase and technology changes, active solar technology may be more effective.

Passive solar design is very useful. The Shelter Institute in Bath, Maine, runs seminars in house building that emphasize passive solar design. They concentrate on:

- Siting a house to take advantage of hills to the north, sheltering trees as windbreaks and sun shade.
- Locating windows so that they are exposed to winter sun but shaded in the summer when the leaves are out.
- Making windows so that they are sealed where necessary.
- Organizing a careful balance and proper locations for insulation and ventilation.
- Locating the front door so that northern winds cannot blow directly into the library and there is a lobby weather baffle, or offset double doors.

Many of these principles are applicable to the design of libraries. However, in larger buildings there are other considerations. Materials may themselves provide useful insulating mass. People and lighting supply considerable heat, and lighting may be a significant energy consumer and require additional cooling power.

Air conditioning in the summer often costs more than winter heating and also benefits from insulation. Several improvements in air conditioning have been made. Economizer controls permit increased use of outside air for cooling in the spring and fall. Heat pumps provide lower cost and more versatility where electrical rates are low. Variable air volume control systems provide increased control in large areas and often reduce the size of the air conditioning units required. Four pipe systems provide the flexibility to heat and cool different areas at the same time. Hybrid air conditioning systems using through-wall perimeter units and a smaller central unit offer increased flexibility and the possibility of some cooling when the central system breaks down. They may also reduce installation and operating costs in medium-sized systems.

Here are some questions to ask and things to look for in discussing HVAC with your architect and mechanical engineer:

- Where are the thermostats? They should be located where people are sitting and working and never where the sun can strike them directly.
- Where is the entrance? Does it face north? Is there a wind and temperature baffle?
- Where are the air conditioning units and fans? Is there room to reach them for maintenance?
- How thick is the insulation? 12 inches on ceiling, 4 inches on walls is required.
- Where are the windows in relation to north? How will seating areas near windows be heated and cooled? Direct sunlight should *never* fall on long-term seating areas.
- What will it take to heat, cool, and light this building? Federal standards require that buildings use no more than 80,000 BTUs per square foot per year. Lighting should not require more than two watts per square foot.

Energy conservation features to be considered:

- Offset entry locks reduce the amount of heat or cool air lost at the entry of the building.
- Passive insulation—large masses surrounding the building such as

berm buildings, underground buildings, or buildings with thick earth coverings on the roof—provide stabilized temperatures.

- Window wells—instead of the windows looking directly out on an area where air could blow into the window, the windows are let down into the earth in light wells below ground level so that the air is more controlled, and does not blow directly onto the window.

- Economizer controls in air conditioning use large percentages of outside air in spring and fall. In summer, cool night air is brought into the building in quantities to cool it down in the evening.

- Building orientation with windows pointed south and blank walls north.

- Thermostats are necessary for all office and small room spaces, with exception of storage areas and closets.

- In winter, cold outdoor air is brought into the building only through ducts that are solar heated so that fresh air enters only after it is heated.

- Heavy oil, used as an inexpensive heating source, preheated by solar systems so that the oil is already very warm when it gets to the oil burner.

- Lighting can be used to assist in heating outside air as well as being designed in a task mode, so that instead of general lighting, which could consume as much as 2 watts per square foot, task lighting can be used, which would bring that consumption down to one half watt per square foot.

- Variable volume air conditioning should be considered as it offers useful flexibility and good economy.

- Zone controls for program, children's, technical, and administration areas will be necessary.

- Zone controls should be used for heating and air conditioning on day, night, and holiday cycles.

8

Putting Plans Together

A recent library effectiveness survey of library users showed that among others these were considered "effectiveness factors of major importance" and related to building location and design. (Numbers relate to library user ratings.)

6. Convenience of location
7. Materials availability
11. Parking
19. Building suitability
21. Building easy to identify
22. Flexibility

From: *Public Library Effectiveness Study* by Thomas Childers & Nancy Van House, 1989

SITE

If convenience of location is the most important building consideration, it is vital that long-term consideration be devoted to site.

Before the advent of shopping malls located on the outskirts of towns and cities, it was a relatively straightforward matter to locate libraries. Consultants advised center of town retail locations. Today, selecting a library site has become a much more complex decision. In medium-sized towns of 20,000 to 100,000 people, downtown is seldom visited by the affluent well-educated typical library user.

A massive mall culture has developed and libraries must consider some form of presence at the mall. This may take the form of a small porta-kiosk structure, a medium-sized store location, or even one of the larger mall anchor stores. It may well be argued that a major library anchor in a mall should command a low rental since it is an ideal loss leader, giving a universally useful product at the lowest possible price.

Convincing trustees and town officials to locate a library at a mall is a tough job. Most trustees and town officials see libraries as precious temples of learning that belong in the now-deserted town center across from the green or in a parklike setting, not where crowds of people come. On the other hand, it is hard to predict the future of malls. Shopping patterns change. Massive efforts are being made to attract people back downtown. A mall is often on the periphery of a town, and, as competing malls develop on opposite sides of town, shopping patterns change. In the late 1990s gas shortages and the revival of mass transportation may change library site preference in favor of downtown locations.

Recently consultants have been more concerned with parking convenience than with location. The ability to park and conveniently reach the library with an armload of books may be as important as a downtown site. Steeply sloping parking lots, underground or tiered parking, and isolated back road locations are to be avoided.

Criteria for a Library Site

Towns build libraries very infrequently, on the average about once in forty years, yet they will be used by more citizens than any other building in town. Libraries are used by children, students, businesspeople, do-it-yourselfers, artists, writers, taxpayers, people learning new skills, professionals updating their knowledge. The library must be in a location where it can be constantly visible to all of these people. A good location is

- On a major road used by most citizens.
- Near a shopping center that is open nights and Saturdays when the library will be open.
- Near parking and mass transportation.
- Easy for pedestrians and children on bicycles to find, and safe for them to come to (safe traffic control).

- Convenient for the elderly and handicapped—no curbs, or at least curb cuts, no hills from the parking lot to the library.

Locations to avoid are

- *Parks*, which are dangerous at night, subject to vandalism
- *Schools*, close in mid-afternoon and are noisy. Most town residents do not attend school.
- *Offices* are closed at night, crowded and noisy in daytime.
- *Town Halls* or *civic centers* are often closed at night.

Site cost is usually a minor fraction of construction and operating costs, yet if the library is obscurely located it will not be used and the people will be paying for a facility that is inconvenient for them. A library is built for citizen *use*—if people see it, they will use it. Ninety-five percent of present library use is by automobile so accessibility will depend on access from the major town road and sufficient parking.

Two percent of a town budget is spent annually to operate a library; if it is visible, people will use it. It will cost $1 million (or more) for a building. Make sure it will be used.

PARKING

Parking can often be the life blood for suburban libraries. Parking requirements can be determined in several different ways:

- Building size is often the criterion used by town zoning agencies, with 350 to 500 square feet of building per parking space.
- Reader seats and meeting room seats can be determinants.
- Surveys of pedestrian versus vehicular use can be a consideration.
- One space for every 300 square feet or one space for every two readers' seats.

Spaces should be nine feet wide except where small car marking is permitted. However, in unattended parking lots small car spaces cannot be controlled and may result in damage. Snow plowing access should be considered as well as snow stacking space. Colored curb cuts for handicapped access and convenient location to library entrance without steep slopes should also be considered.

BUILDING LEVELS

Advantages of a Single-Story Library

Better Service. Staff supervision in a single-story library is more effective, since supervisors can monitor the whole staff.

Easier to Use. Public orientation to single-story libraries is simpler because all parts of the library can be seen at one time. Materials on non-entry levels of a multistory library are not visible to the public on entering the building.

Lower Cost. Elevators are costly to install and maintain and they require waiting. Thus, a single-story library produces higher staff efficiency, lower maintenance, and lower utility costs.

Better Use of Materials. When all materials are on the entry level they will be equally accessible. Multistory libraries with materials on different levels tend to result in lesser use for materials on non-entry levels.

Staff Flexibility. All library personnel can be used interchangeably to provide public services on demand, while in multistory libraries some staff members may be swamped, with the public waiting in line for help while staff members on other floors are idle.

Better Security. Security of materials and staff is better in a single-story building because all staff members are able to assist in supervising and controlling public activities. In a multistory library, supervision requires more staff and one staff member cannot always immediately come to the assistance of another when there is a problem.

Vertical Locations

Up to a maximum of fifteen to twenty thousand square feet, a single-story library works well. Beyond this size advantages are less definite since a larger staff is needed at this scale of service. The Thousand Oaks, California, library has sixty thousand square feet on one floor but has the advantage of an elevated parking lot and a downward sloping interior entrance ramp providing a useful orienting view as the user enters.

It is often useful in programming to separate vertical locations into two categories:

Entrance Level Functions. These must include the most heavily used activities, since it would be inefficient and disturbing to require users to travel through little-used quiet areas to reach heavily used noisy areas.

- Circulation work area and check-in/out
- New materials
- Recent magazines and newspapers
- Reference information center should be near nonfiction books, which are often useful in answering questions
- Reference books and work stations
- Fiction and nonfiction books—fiction books may be located near new books or on another level.
- An entry-level location is preferred for children's services and young adult services, but they may be located on another level if they require a large area and are separately staffed. They should if at all possible be on the same level as adult services in order to encourage children and adults to take an interest in one another's library activities.

Other Level Functions.

- Program and meeting rooms
- Heating, ventilating, air conditioning
- Maintenance
- Administration
- Technical services

LIBRARY BUILDING ANALYSIS

Functional

Area Sizes and Relationships

Libraries may be usefully analyzed by percentage of space required for functions within each area.

I. Public service areas   45–55%

    Circulation – Browsing   1%
    Information – Reference   3%
    40% Adult
    Fiction books   10%
    Nonfiction books   20%
    Video – Audio   3%
    Reading – Study   5%

    7% Children
    Preschool   3%
    Staff work   1%
    Study – Reference   2%
    Story hour   1%

II. Staff work areas   20–25%

    Administration
    Technical services
    Storage

III. Nonassignable   25–30%

    Heating
    Air conditioning
    Stairs & elevators
    Walls
    Corridors

By Function

Assignable	65–80%
Books, materials	40–50%
Seats	10–20%
Programs	5–10%
Staff work	20–25%
Nonassignable	25–30%
Heating	
Air conditioning	
Stairs & elevators	
Toilets	
Storage	
Walls	
Corridors	

Library Service   55–60%

Adult		35%
Fiction		5%
Nonfiction		25%
Reference		3%
Periodicals		2%
Program	Multipurpose	5%
Children's		12%
Preschool		
Story hour		
Young adult		3%

Staff Function   20%

Staff	5%
Technical services	5%
Administration	3%
Staff lounge – Lunch room	2%
Custodial	
Storage	5%
Lockers	
Restrooms	

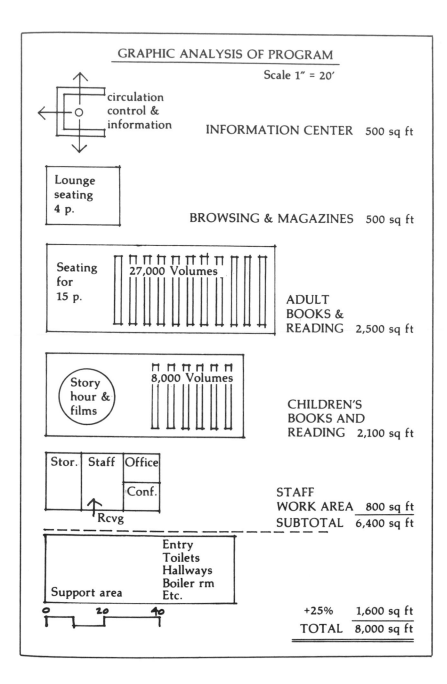

GRAPHIC ANALYSIS OF PROGRAM

Scale 1" = 20'

circulation control & information

INFORMATION CENTER   500 sq ft

Lounge seating 4 p.

BROWSING & MAGAZINES   500 sq ft

Seating for 15 p.

27,000 Volumes

ADULT BOOKS & READING   2,500 sq ft

Story hour & films

8,000 Volumes

CHILDREN'S BOOKS AND READING   2,100 sq ft

Stor. | Staff | Office

Conf.

Rcvg

STAFF WORK AREA   800 sq ft
SUBTOTAL   6,400 sq ft

Entry
Toilets
Hallways
Boiler rm
Etc.

Support area

0   20   40

+25%   1,600 sq ft
TOTAL   8,000 sq ft

PUTTING THE LIBRARY TOGETHER

The user experience of public libraries differs significantly from that of school and college libraries in that the majority of public library users visit less frequently. Consequently, entrance orientation for services and self-service design becomes more vital.

The Entrance Experience

The most heavily used materials should be placed near the entrance. Recent books and magazines should be clearly identified by spotlighting and graphics and spread out on display shelving for multiple user access. A reference library service center should have several self-service computer work stations with printers providing:

- Bibliographic access to library materials
- Bibliographic access to other libraries
- In-house full-text access
- Remote full-text access
- Reference librarian assistance
- Reference books and vertical files
- Magazine indexes and back issues

Nonfiction books should be nearby to help in answering reference questions.

Reading Areas

Reading areas should contain:

- Stand-up short-term use index and reference books
- Oversized newspaper tables
- Lounge-style magazine chairs
- Carrels for long term use in quiet isolated locations
- Group study rooms

Acoustical separation of noisy entrance and staff service areas from quiet, long-term use areas can be accomplished by sound absorbing finishes and sound barriers such as tall bookstacks.

Staff Experience

Controlling and servicing collections and public are staff responsibilities requiring the following design characteristics and juxtapositions.

- Check-in and check-out areas near entrance and exit
- Circulation staff work areas near circulation public service area
- Reference staff work areas near reference public service area
- Clear view of stack aisles and reading areas for easy supervision
- Reference proximity to public computer work stations for easy staff assistance
- Copy and fax machines near staff service areas for control and public assistance

The following plan shows, in very simplified form, how the public services of a small branch library serving three thousand people might be juxtaposed.

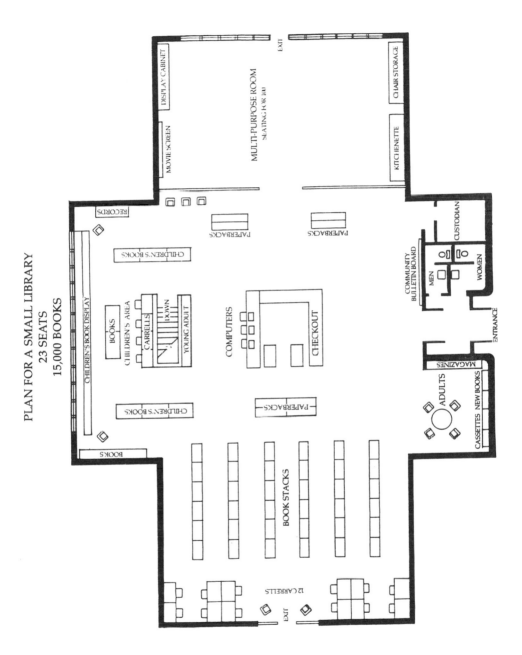

PLAN FOR A SMALL LIBRARY
23 SEATS
15,000 BOOKS

9

Plan Reviews—Design Examples

PLAN REVIEWS

A crucial step in the planning process occurs when the architect draws schematic plans showing how the program will look as a building. These schematic drawings should be to scale and indicate proximities of major functions.

Capacities for books and seating in each functional area should be calculated by the architect and shown on the schematic plan. The consultant and library staff should verify these capacities by measuring the plans and then reviewing them from the point of view of user and staff.

Schematic plans may start as bubble diagrams suggesting proximities and relative sizes. The next step may be to relate boxes scaled to the sizes of functional areas. Finally, schematics will show the footprint—the area that the building occupies on the site. Some architects will even show bookstacks, tables, chairs, and staff work equipment at this step. In designing libraries it is essential that each piece of furniture for public and staff use as well as equipment be drawn on the plan in an early schematic phase, since shapes of functional areas are often set at this time. Bookstacks, chairs, tables, and technical equipment are available in a narrow range of particular sizes. These sizes will determine if the shape of an area is workable for a library function. For example, a long, narrow shape may contain the necessary square footage, yet be too narrow to accommodate the chairs and tables required by the program.

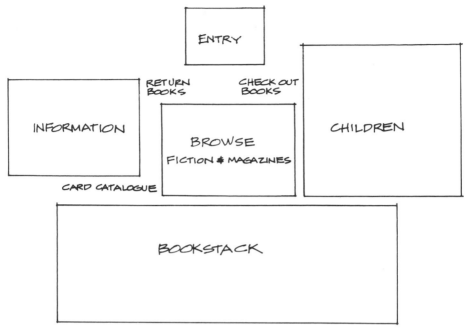

Functional relationships drawn to scale for a building program. Sequence of use: (1) Enter the building; (2) return books; (3) browse in fiction and recent books, look at a newspaper or magazine; (4) inquire at the information desk or look in the card catalog; (5) search for a particular book in the bookstack; (6) check-out a book, leave the building.

Comparing plan and actual function is the process that occurs in plan reviews. This should be done from several points of view:

The user sequence indicates how a library user gets from a parked car to the library entrance with an armload of books, returns the books, finds other materials, checks them out, and exits.

There are no obstacles to entering commercial buildings. We expect treadle operated doors in supermarkets; why not in libraries? The shopper carries parcels; the library user carries books, films, or other circulating materials. The path from parking space or sidewalk to entrance should be as direct as possible. The public must be able to see the entrance from the parking area. The library user should see the entrance rather than be faced with a twisting walk around a series of corners. Some other considerations follow:

- Are parking spaces unnecessarily far from the entrance? Is the slope from the parking lot to the library more than ten percent? Is the entrance clearly visible and inviting?

- When users enter the library, can they understand the layout? Are books visible and arranged in a clear and simple order? Are new materials displayed with the covers out near the entrance? Are reference librarians near the entrance?
- Are audio and visual materials immediately available without time-consuming box matching or asking for staff assistance?
- Are readers offered a sufficiently wide variety of comfortable seats?
- Are chairs shaped with lower lumbar support and curved backs? Can they easily slide on carpets?
- Do chairs swivel and tilt? Are multipurpose tables large enough to be used by several people?
- Are there study carrels in quiet spaces far from noisy staff service areas and entrance? Are there oversized tables near the newspapers?
- Are computer work stations available for the public? Is staff assistance nearby?
- Are children's services near the entrance?
- Are adult seats available in the children's area?
- Are story hour facilities available in the children's area and acoustically separated from children's study areas?
- Do children have a choice of single or group seating, quiet study areas, and search areas?

The staff service sequence provides a variety of library services:

- Finding a book
- Answering a reference question
- Checking out materials
- Supervising public use of library services
- Ordering and processing new materials
- Security of valuable materials

Flexibility and expansion capabilities are analyzed in terms of the inevitable changes rapidly taking place in libraries, such as:

- Automation of library procedures
- CD room and online database access for staff
- Changes in material format (records to CD's, VCR's, micro-materials, and high-density storage)
- Population and service increases

- Children, young adult, aging population requirements

The next expansion to the library should be an integral part of the initial plan.

Accessibility and Convenience

A library and its resources and programs should be accessible and convenient. Planning for this begins with site selection and extends through building design and into the selection of furnishings and equipment. A library should be easy to find, easy to enter, and easy to use.

- Are there multipurpose facilities for library programs as well as small group meeting rooms available when the rest of the library is closed? Is the graphic system coordinated with lighting for effective self-service? Are sign sizes proportional to distance from users, and are signs sequentially positioned to make self-service work?
- Are circulation areas designed in detail for efficient use of circulation systems now and flexibility for the future?

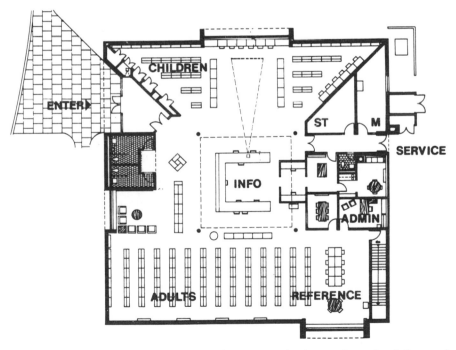

A multistaff information center library showing projection station, circulation and reference functions, as well as staff office, meeting room, and control. Manross Library, Bristol Connecticut, SMS Architects, Willis N. Mills, Jr.

- Are technical service areas designed efficiently for rapid processing of library materials?
- Is there room for book trucks?
- Does the design of work stations allow for individual flexibility?

Design development plans follow final schematics. At this stage architects design the shape of the building and exterior elevations and determine heating, ventilating, and air conditioning machinery locations. Functions become fixed and sizes and relationship changes become complex and time consuming for the architect. Sizes and locations of library public service counters, bookstacks, and chairs and tables are fixed during this stage and equipment selection concerns begin to emerge.

Design development reviews should follow the same pattern as in schematic reviews but now the size, location, and juxtaposition of each item is finally determined and detailed dimensions become more important.

Furniture and equipment recommendations should be made before working drawings commence to assure that dimensions are accurate and equipment will fit comfortably into assigned spaces.

Lighting and graphics recommendations must be made before work begins on working drawings to assure that graphics are well lighted and appropriately placed.

Chairs

In selecting library chairs, several characteristics should be considered:

Durability. Hundreds of people will be using the chairs and it is therefore important to select fabric materials and structure that will last a long time. Wood frames should be carefully examined for their construction before a decision is made as to their durability.

Comfort. People spend a great deal of time in library chairs. Therefore, they should be extremely comfortable and conform to the human body. Several manufacturers now make ergonomically designed chairs. These chairs not only conform to the curve of the back but also provide side-to-side support for the lower back. It is also important that a chair be easy to get into and out of. Older people often have difficulty arising from a comfortable lounge-type chair. People vary in size, so a variety of chair designs may be useful.

Costs. It is, of course, very important to get good value for your money. Library chairs tend to last thirty to forty years in regular use, twelve hours a day, seven days a week. It is difficult to get an inexpensive chair that will hold up and still be handsome over that span of time. The lounge chair designed by Charles Eames is an example of the kind of quality furniture that will last for over twenty years with reupholstering. Woven nylon fabric covered chairs tend to be more breathable and comfortable than vinyl covered chairs.

Carpet Design. In order to move chairs easily on carpeting, they should be light and have some sort of runner on the bottom so that they can slide on the carpet without having to be picked up. The Marcel Breuer design for a side chair is one example. This bent chrome chair will last a long time, is comfortable to sit in, and comes in a wide variety of durable fabrics.

Lounge Chairs. The J. B. Ekornes Company of Norway manufactures a stressless reclining chair and footstool constructed of tubular steel with a leather upholstered, curved foam back. This is an extremely comfortable chair that can be easily adjusted, fit any size person and is relatively easy to get into and out of. It has an important additional advantage in that a spare set of cushions can be purchased and installed immediately if the upholstery is damaged, thus retaining use of the chair.

Other chair manufacturers to consider are Steelcase (Sensor office chair), Jasper wooden chairs, Thonet, and Wieland (manufactures lounge seating with velcro for easy reupholstering).

Creativity, Ingenuity, and Design

After all the structure and detail of planning a complex library, user satisfaction with that library will continue to depend on how people perceive it, and feel about it, in addition to how well it functions.

The planning process should depend heavily on input from the staff and community. We believe that the process of planning a new library in the 1990s is, to paraphrase Ken Dowlin, like trying to design a car as it accelerates rolling down a hill. If this is so, then we must look outside the community and beyond existing models to try to create libraries that will respond in ways quite different from the old ways to a whole new array of needs. How can this be done?

There are two different definitions of creativity. One emphasizes the departure from prior knowledge or procedure, creating by intuitively coming up with a solution that no prior knowledge or learned process can completely explain. The other definition emphasizes the combining of two earlier existing concepts in a new way. This creativity can be encouraged in several ways:

Library visits by staff, trustees, architects, and consultants are vital in stimulating new thinking. All too many new libraries are programmed and designed to solve the problems of an existing library building planned twenty to forty years ago with little attention paid to how newer buildings are designed and how future problems can be solved.

Brain-storming, charettes, focus groups by staff, users, trustees, architects. Several architectural firms develop this process, which must be carefully distinguished from designing by committee. A skilled designer can have dialogue with a group by visiting another library with them, showing slides of, or discussing, various design solutions to programmatic needs.

Library Visits

Improvement alternatives are often suggested by the library consultant, who is more knowledgeable in this area than the librarian or committee. However, it is important not only to judge the level of the consultant's expertise but also to understand the variety of possible solutions. Library literature can be helpful. *Library Journal* and *American Libraries,* for example, publish annual issues on new library buildings, and the American Library Association sponsors a biennial architectural competition in collaboration with the AIA, American Institute of Architects.

Your own photographs taken during trips visiting new library buildings can be shared by all committee members. Here are some things to look for in new buildings:

- Is there an exterior sign telling the library hours? Is it lit internally or externally? Can it be seen from cars?
- Location: near shopping or community facilities that are open during library hours? Was the library easy to find?
- Parking and public transportation: was it easy to park? Was a bus stop nearby?
- Entrance: is it convenient to go from the parking lot into the building?
- Barrier-free access for the handicapped? Handicapped parking near the building? Was there a ramped curb? Handrails? Are the doors easy to operate by the handicapped? Can you get through the doors easily?

- Are the library's hours of service prominently displayed on a sign and at the entry?
- When you enter the library, do you know where to go?
- Can each functional area be seen from the entrance?
- Are directional signs easy to see and logical to follow?

Children/Adults	Catalog
Books/Other Media	Reference/Information

- Is there easy access to a public telephone (low for handicapped) and copy machine? Is there a public telephone outside?
- Does there seem to be sufficient and appropriate space available to offer full range of programs?
- Is there an auditorium, multipurpose room?
- Is storytelling area in or adjacent to children's room, but out of the traffic flow?
- Are there display and exhibit areas? Are they highly visible? Accessible, with special lighting? Are they secure? Controlled from staff station?
- Are these functions visible from staff stations?

Books – Materials
Reading – Users – Media
Staff – Communications – Reference

- Does there appear to be effective traffic flow?
- Where is the online Public Access or card catalog? Is it accesible to staff and public? Near reference and nonfiction? Is it accessible from both circulation desk and reference desk? Are additional terminals strategically located?
- Are all public areas accessible to handicapped users with ramps or elevators, wide aisles, easy doors?

Toilet Facilities.

- Are they adequate?
- Are there rails and a wide area for the handicapped? Stainless mirrors?
- Are they easy to find without asking?
- Are they controllable and well lighted?

Circulation Area. Examine this area carefully as it is a major contact point between the staff and the library user. This location should provide visual and functional control of public areas. Notice carefully which functions and routines are located here.

- Are the functions logically arranged and identified?
- Is the arrangement convenient for the user?
- Are returns and check-out areas separated?
- Is there a registration and inquiry area?
- Can books be returned immediately at entrance?
- Do books and other library materials circulate with minimal fuss?
- Are the materials transferred easily to their correct locations? Can they be immediately checked out again? Note the space allocated to this central function. Is it too large, too small?
- Is there room to expand as circulation of materials increases?
- Is there smooth handling of all user requirements, even during maximum-use periods? This requires several flexible staff locations.

Reference-Information Area.

- Is it near the catalog or terminals?
- Is it near the reference books?
- Is there seating for public and staff communication?
- Is lighting adequate for small type and glossy pages?
- Are there provisions for future terminals, microreaders, and other machines?
- Is there an audiovisual area nearby?
- Can individuals readily use the media?
- Are there adequate electrical receptacles?
- Are indexes, reference periodicals, microreaders and materials grouped conveniently and near current periodicals?
- Is there carrel seating for users right near the reference materials?
- Is there acoustical treatment—acoustical ceilings, partitions, carpeting-to dampen sound in this area?
- Is there a quiet study area?
- Is there a small meeting room in this area?
- Is there a staff work area nearby?

Children's Facilities.

- Is there a welcoming, comfortable section of the room instantly perceivable, yet outside of the main "hurly-burly" traffic flow, for the picture book age child?
- Is there furniture for this size child?
- Is there also a comfortable place for an adult to sit while sharing a book with the young child?
- Are there touchable objects to attract the young child? Are they sturdy enough for touching?
- Is the progression by subject clear?
- Are audiovisual materials and equipment in evidence?
- Are there toys, games and realia? Display bulletin boards with lighting?
- Is there a discernible warmth and welcome in the children's room?
- What is the relationship of the stack area to seating space? Depressing or inviting? Open or crowded? Top heavy or well spaced?
- Is there an eye-catching space for a story hour or other programming?

Seating. Does the seating appear to be adequate: comfortable back support, upholstery, light? Are the chairs easy to get out of?

Bookstacks. Allow the top and bottom shelves to remain empty for future expansion.

- Are the books well maintained (plastic covers, rebinding)?
- Are the stacks arranged in one numerical sequence so that the user can find the material without having to ask?
- Are there end signs, shelf labels, Dewey break locators?
- Are the bottom-shelf books well lighted without glare?
- Are the most popular materials (new books, for example) conveniently located?
- Are special collections identified?
- Are conditions appropriate for adequate care and maintenance of rare material? Is there climate control? Humidity control? Space for growth? Natural light control?
- Is this collection available to the public? How? What are the control and access mechanisms?

Noise Control. Acoustical separation of public areas from staff work areas is essential for noise control. Areas designated for quiet study (reference area, study carrels) should be away from main traffic patterns but accessible. The circulation desk area is the noisiest. This is as it should be; in fact, maximum communication between staff and users at this service point should be encouraged. Is there acoustical ceiling tile? Acoustical enclosures for machines? Is there carpeting? Bookstacks are excellent noise absorbers.

Nonpublic Areas. The workroom, near information or card catalog, is for processing and audio-visual work.

- Is there adequate space for smooth function of current activities?
- Has space been reserved for staff or services expansion? The major staff workroom should be located near the circulation desk.
- Is there a variety of storage areas near activities? How is it used? Is it needed? Try to anticipate future storage needs, for gifts and duplicate periodicals, for example.

Mechanicals.

- Is the wiring adequate? Is there extra electrical service capacity?
- Are there empty conduits for phones, speakers, basic audio-visual functions, and for cable television and terminals?
- Is there computer capacity in a cool location free of static?
- Is there humidity control?
- Are all windows functional? This is especially important in New England. Weather conditions might permit shutting off of both heat and air conditioning for four to six months of the year, for good conservation of energy.
- Where are the thermostats?
- Can lighting be moved?

Are areas defined by their lighting? Notice particularly stack lighting and lighting level in reference area. Is there variety and color? Are the lights easily controlled? Be aware that different intensities of lighting are appropriate to different areas of the library.

The Future.

- Is expansion on the present site possible?

- Who has title to the land?
- Is adjacent land available for future purchase?
- Is expansion inside the building possible?
- What is floor load for compact shelving?

Adaptive Reuse

Adaptive reuse of existing buildings in older built-up communities often makes use of an attractive site and is sometimes a useful political solution in towns where schools, town halls, or other municipal and commercial facilities become available. Of course, a major obstacle to using such structures for library purposes is the 150-pound per square foot structural load-bearing capacity necessary for fully loaded 90-inch-high bookstacks. Buildings can often be reinforced structurally and it is possible, though not recommended, to configure lower widely spaced stacks for lower structural capacities. Buildings with single levels built on grade (on the ground) usually can support the weight of books, but even these should be checked for ground stability, especially if heavier high-density storage stacks requiring 300 pounds per square foot load capacity are contemplated.

Parking convenience is always a consideration and in adaptive reuse may be a deciding factor. The location, as in the case of schools, is often away from town centers or retail locations and can be a less attractive library location in spite of parking convenience—especially after the year 2000, when single-person automobile use may be more restrictive. Supermarkets, on the other hand, are much better adaptive reuse candidates than schools. They are usually located on busy roads, require minimal structural change, and have open flexible plans, unlike chopped up classroom spaces, and they are therefore relatively inexpensive to convert.

Conversion costs are extraordinarily difficult to predict, requiring a wider margin of error than estimates for new buildings because of the inaccuracy of as-built plans and the obsolescence of much mechanical HVAC equipment. A school conversion in Barrington, Rhode Island, and a supermarket in Marshfield, Massachusetts, are examples of successful conversions.

Design Examples

Dual-function buildings in Coventry, Rhode Island, and King-of-Prussia, Pennsylvania, are examples of successful public library-town hall combinations. Some advantages include dual-purpose parking (daytime sharing with the town hall, evening for library use); public dual-purpose convenience; slightly lower cost by combining design and building costs and sharing location, land acquisition, and site development costs. Disadvantages include competition for day parking convenience and expansion constraints and competition. Evening isolation may also be a consideration if the neighborhood is an office area that shuts down after 5:00 PM. Libraries are heavily used in the evening and on weekends and should be located in areas where evening and weekend activities take place.

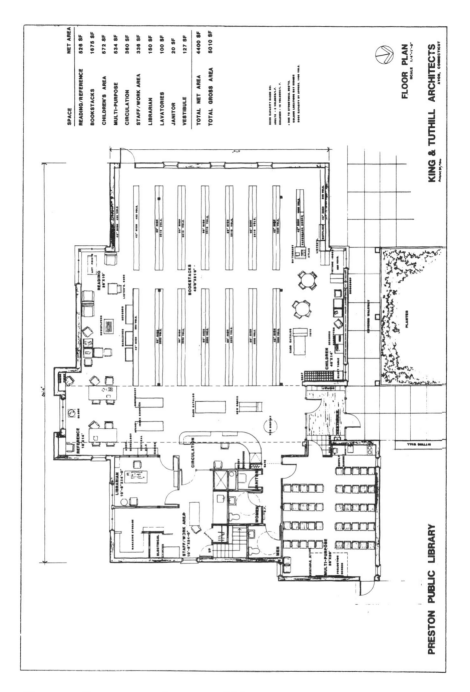

SPACE	NET AREA
READING/REFERENCE	526 SF
BOOKSTACKS	1675 SF
CHILDREN'S AREA	572 SF
MULTI-PURPOSE	534 SF
CIRCULATION	360 SF
STAFF/WORK AREA	336 SF
LIBRARIAN	150 SF
LAVATORIES	100 SF
JANITOR	20 SF
VESTIBULE	127 SF
TOTAL NET AREA	4400 SF
TOTAL GROSS AREA	5010 SF

FLOOR PLAN
SCALE 1/4"=1'-0"

KING & TUTHILL ARCHITECTS
AVON, CONNECTICUT

PRESTON PUBLIC LIBRARY

Preston, Connecticut, has a small library designed by Charles King for single staff member operation in a community of three thousand in rural New England. A shared central bookstack separates the children's area at the entrance from the quiet adult area at the rear, and a central staff circulation-reference desk is convenient to the staff work area.

99

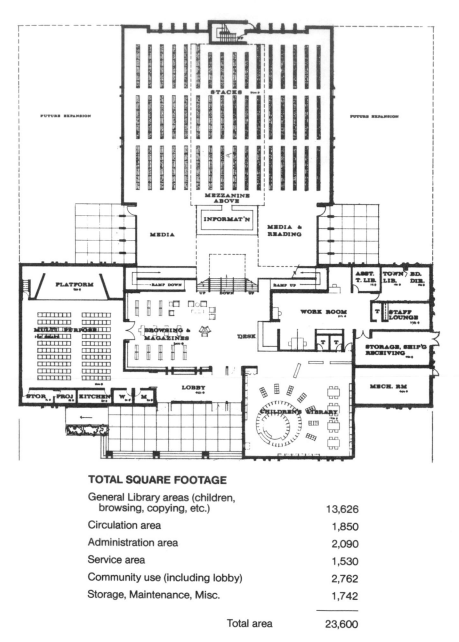

TOTAL SQUARE FOOTAGE

General Library areas (children, browsing, copying, etc.)	13,626
Circulation area	1,850
Administration area	2,090
Service area	1,530
Community use (including lobby)	2,762
Storage, Maintenance, Misc.	1,742
Total area	23,600

Trumbull, Connecticut library plans called for future expansion in the stacks and reading areas. An unusual feature is the location of the multipurpose area with large double-opening doors for temporary use as a study area during busy times. The children's area designed in 1974 proved to be much too small for the expanding children's population of the 1980s and was difficult to expand in its existing location. Circulation and information functions were well located for supervision of public areas.

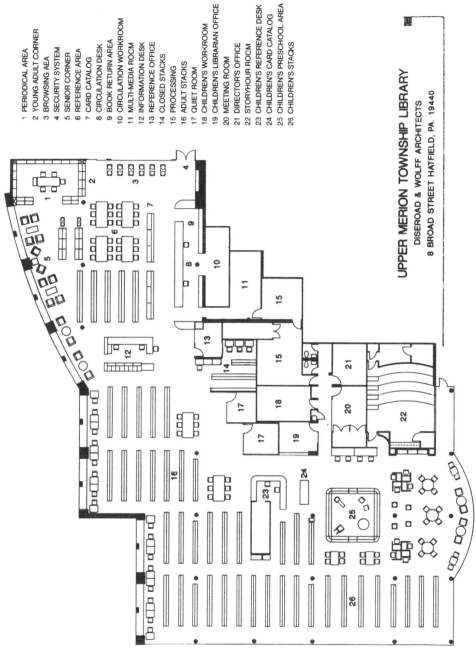

1 PERIODICAL AREA
2 YOUNG ADULT CORNER
3 BROWSING AEA
4 SECURITY SYSTEM
5 SENIOR CORNER
6 REFERENCE AREA
7 CARD CATALOG
8 CIRCULATION DESK
9 BOOK RETURN AREA
10 CIRCULATION WORKROOM
11 MULTI-MEDIA ROOM
12 INFORMATION DESK
13 REFERENCE OFFICE
14 CLOSED STACKS
15 PROCESSING
16 ADULT STACKS
17 QUIET ROOM
18 CHILDREN'S WORKROOM
19 CHILDREN'S LIBRARIAN OFFICE
20 MEETING ROOM
21 DIRECTOR'S OFFICE
22 STORYHOUR ROOM
23 CHILDREN'S REFERENCE DESK
24 CHILDREN'S CARD CATALOG
25 CHILDREN'S PRESCHOOL AREA
26 CHILDREN'S STACKS

UPPER MERION TOWNSHIP LIBRARY
DISEROAD & WOLFF ARCHITECTS
8 BROAD STREET HATFIELD, PA. 19440

This plan for Upper Merion, Pennsylvania, prepared by Diseroad & Wolff is part of a multilevel municipal complex. It features an open, flexible plan with central linked adult, children's service, and staff support areas. Bookstacks can be easily expanded for children and adults, and there is a wide range of peripheral seating. The children's library is unusually large and includes a sound insulated story hour room.

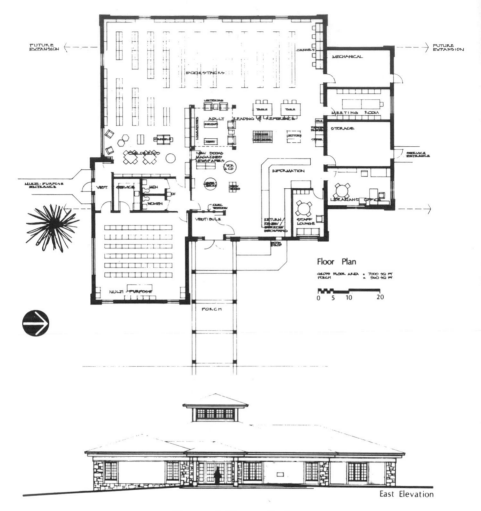

Floor Plan

East Elevation

Prospect, Connecticut.

Richard Schoenhardt has extensive experience in the design of small libraries, and this plan provides for an information-circulation area with reading and browsing and a multipurpose room accessible separately.

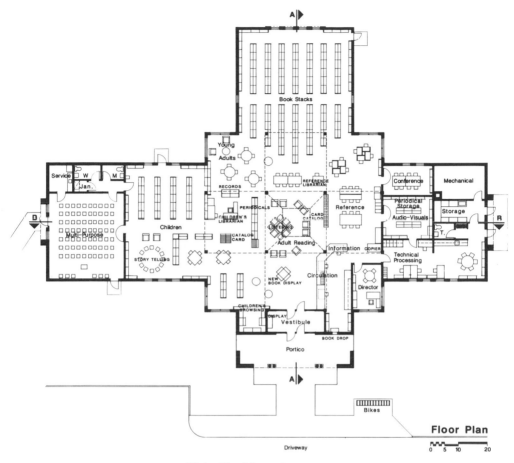

Plainville, Massachusetts.

The library at Plainville, Massachusetts is located on a 200-by-200-foot portion of the front lawn of the Wood School, and positioned so as to not block a view from the street to the school. A thirty-two-car parking lot partially surrounded by new shade trees provides for convenient automobile access and includes spaces for handicapped persons. The site area allows for a possible future addition of 3,000 square feet. The interior features high central spaces and cozy lower ceiling alcoves along north and south sides. The children's area is separated by window walls to provide acoustical control. Children have two window seat alcoves for reading. Included is a multipurpose room that has seating for forty-nine persons. The plan is efficient, easy to manage and capable of expansion to the west if needed. This library was also designed by Richard Schoenhardt.

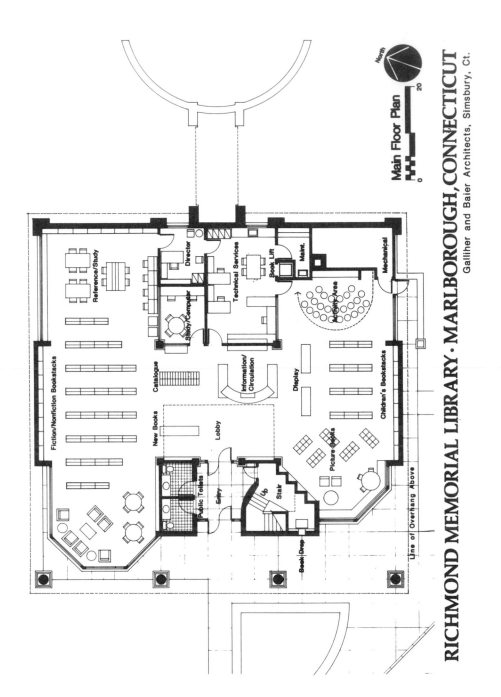

RICHMOND MEMORIAL LIBRARY · MARLBOROUGH, CONNECTICUT

Galliher and Baier Architects, Simsbury, Ct.

Main Floor Plan

North

An interesting small library designed by Norman Baier with symmetrical children's and adult wings has an upper story multi-purpose and storage area.

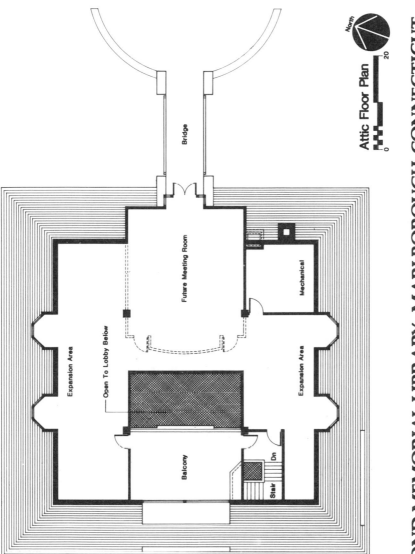

Attic Floor Plan

North

0 20

Bridge

Future Meeting Room

Mechanical

Expansion Area

Open To Lobby Below

Expansion Area

Balcony

Stair

Dn

RICHMOND MEMORIAL LIBRARY · MARLBOROUGH, CONNECTICUT

Galliher and Baier Architects, Simsbury, Ct.

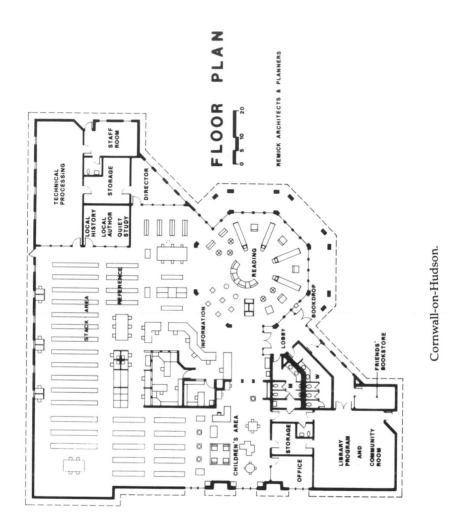

FLOOR PLAN

REMICK ARCHITECTS & PLANNERS

0 5 10 20

Cornwall-on-Hudson.

TECHNICAL PROCESSING

STAFF ROOM

STORAGE

DIRECTOR

LOCAL HISTORY

LOCAL AUTHOR

QUIET STUDY

REFERENCE

STACK AREA

READING

INFORMATION

BOOKDROP

LOBBY

FRIENDS' BOOKSTORE

CHILDREN'S AREA

M

W

STORAGE

OFFICE

LIBRARY PROGRAM AND COMMUNITY ROOM

The design by Conrad Remick for Cornwall, New York, includes a central octagonal browsing court, combined circulation-information service and staff work area, and peripheral stacks and study carrels. An exhibit gallery provides separate access to the multipurpose room.

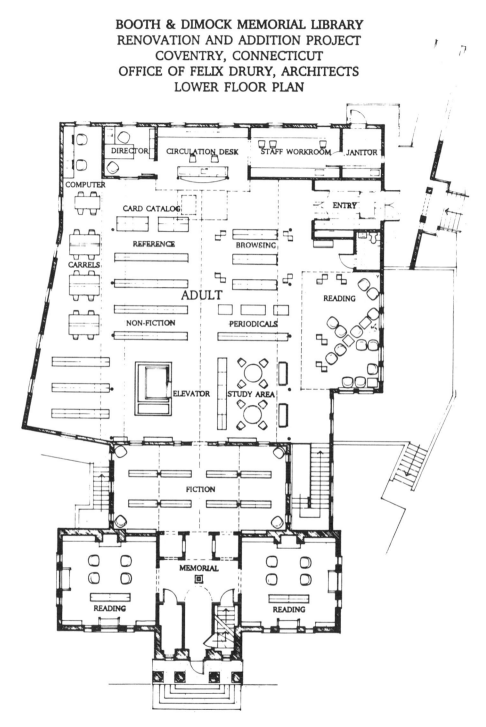

BOOTH & DIMOCK MEMORIAL LIBRARY
RENOVATION AND ADDITION PROJECT
COVENTRY, CONNECTICUT
OFFICE OF FELIX DRURY, ARCHITECTS
LOWER FLOOR PLAN

DIRECTOR · CIRCULATION DESK · STAFF WORKROOM · JANITOR
COMPUTER
CARD CATALOG · ENTRY
REFERENCE · BROWSING
CARRELS
ADULT · READING
NON-FICTION · PERIODICALS
ELEVATOR · STUDY AREA
FICTION
MEMORIAL
READING · READING

A Felix Drury design for a renovation/addition at Coventry, Connecticut, features angled stacks and a large interesting children's services design.

107

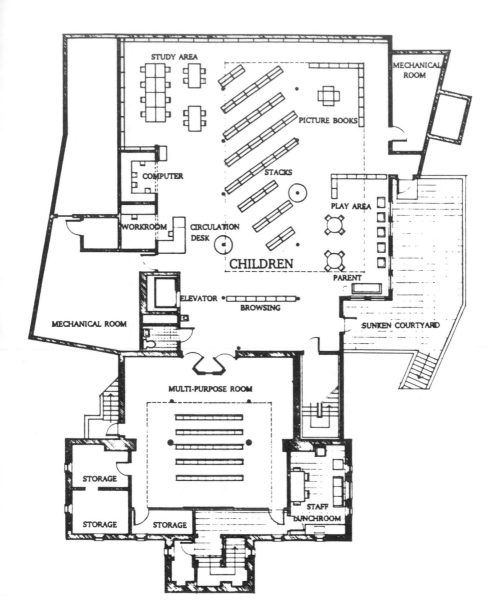

STUDY AREA

MECHANICAL ROOM

PICTURE BOOKS

COMPUTER

STACKS

WORKROOM

CIRCULATION DESK

PLAY AREA

CHILDREN

PARENT

MECHANICAL ROOM

ELEVATOR

BROWSING

SUNKEN COURTYARD

MULTI-PURPOSE ROOM

STORAGE

STORAGE

STORAGE

STAFF LUNCHROOM

BOOTH & DIMOCK MEMORIAL LIBRARY
RENOVATION AND ADDITION PROJECT
COVENTRY, CONNECTICUT
OFFICE OF FELIX DRURY, ARCHITECTS
UPPER FLOOR PLAN

LIBRARY IMPROVEMENT PLANNING ESTIMATES

Public Functions

Seats

> 5 seats per 1,000 population (Wheeler)
> 30 square feet per seat, as an average
> 25 square feet per reader seated at a table
> 15 square feet multi-purpose room seat
> Seat height—15 1/2-18 inches
> Seat depth—15-17 inches

Tables

> Aisle space—5 feet
> Height—30 inches adult; 25 to 28 inches children
> Round—48 or 42 inches for children
> Rectangular—48 × 72 inches for four reader, 90 inches for six

Space Requirements

Seats	*Square feet*
Reading/conference table	25
Lounge seating	50
Carrel or index table	35
Computer readerwork station	50
Seating in auditorium	15
Young children floor seating	10
Four-person table	100
Bench (two seats)	10

Storage	
File cabinet, vertical or lateral	18
Microfilm cabinet	15
Card Catalog:	
free-standing 72-drawer unit	45
built-in 72-drawer unit	21
Files for maps	40

Other Storage

Free standing dictionary stand with user	25
Free standing atlas with user	35
Audio visual cabinet with drawer extended and user	20

Staff

Work station	80
Work station	120
Office/work station for secretary and reception area	150–75 square feet per staff
Office/work station for division head	100–25 square feet per staff
Office area for administrative librarian	125–50 square feet per staff
Office for assistant director	225
Office for director	300

Bookstack Structural Requirements

Dead load-include the weight of the structure itself, i.e., steel concrete, wood, roofing materials, electrical and mechanical systems, doors, windows, and so forth.

Live load-include the weight of the moveable elements, i.e., furniture, shelving, equipment, books, materials, people, and so forth.

Typical live loads are as follows:

80–100 pounds per SF	most office buildings
150 pounds per SF	library general stack area
150–200 pounds per SF	raised floor areas
300 pounds per SF	compact shelving areas
300–500 pounds per SF	library file, record and microfilm storage rooms

The main weight factor in libraries is the weight of the loaded book stack.

Paper weighs 58 pounds per cubic foot and a conventional 90-inch-high double-faced, metal book stack section, 36 inches wide, with fourteen 10-inch-deep shelves, loaded to 85 percent capacity, weighs approximately 1,972 pounds. Fully loaded, it weighs approximately 2,320 pounds.

Floor loading weights can be changed by adjusting the

- height of the shelving and the number of shelves
- types of material being stored
- fullness of the shelves
- spacing or aisle width between book stack ranges.

Library Bookstacks: General Specifications

Scope. This specification covers delivery and installation of steel bookstack shelving of the bracket type only. Unit heights, depths, and accessories shall be as indicated on the plans or schedule of equipment.

Materials and Workmanship. Only the finest materials and quality of workmanship will be acceptable. Sheet material is to be cold rolled, Class I steel. Gauge thicknesses are U.S. standard with the following minimum requirements:

- Upright columns of welded frame: #16 gauge.
- Top and bottom spreaders of welded frame: #16 gauge.
- Shelves (including base shelf): #18 & #19 gauge.
- Shelf-end brackets: #16 gauge.

All shelving shall be carefully adjusted to the floor and leveled. Wall shelving shall be attached to the walls at the most inconspicuous locations.

Type. Steel bookstacks shall be cantilever, unit construction design with individual welded frame assemblies. Starter and adder combinations or welded frame every other unit are not acceptable. Commercial or case-type shelvings will not be considered. The modular construction shall be such that all components of a bookstack section may be removed from any range without in any way disturbing the adjacent units, so that any range may be divided for the purpose of rearrangements without the necessity of procuring additional components. Any bracing that prevents insertion of oversize material past the center line on any base or adjustable shelf is unacceptable.

Individual standard (catalogued) components to be as follows:

Welded Frame. Upright columns of welded frame shall be formed of not less than #16 gauge steel into channel shape with no less than 1/2-inch stiffening flanges measuring 2 inches in the web and 1-1/4 inch at front and rear surfaces. Uprights are to be perforated with a series of 3/16-by-5/8 inch slots spaced 1 inch apart on vertical centers and located within 5/16 inch from the web. Every fifth and sixth slot shall be shaped differently to ease visual leveling of adjustable shelves.

Top spreader of welded frame will consist of not less than #16 gauge tubular steel shape measuring at least 1-by-2-1/2 inches in cross-section. This spreader is to be electrically welded to uprights at concealed locations.

Bottom spreader of welded frame will consist of not less than #16 gauge steel channel shape measuring at least 1-by-1-3/4 inch in cross-section and be equipped with two adjustable neoprene covered glides to provide protection to floor covering and to prevent "walking" of stack units. The outer ends will receive weld nuts predrilled to receive floor leveler glides. Bottom spreader to be electrically welded to uprights, with open portion of channel positioned upward.

Closed Base Support Bracket. Base support brackets shall be designed to fit snugly in and around welded frame upright. Material shall be no less than #16 gauge steel.

Brackets shall have a 90 degree flange at bottom that will rest on floor covering. Capability to level bookstack unit shall be incorporated into the base bracket. Top and front edge of base is to be flanged outward approximately 1/4 inch. Profile of this bracket shall match that of adjustable shelf end bracket and in addition shall have a hole in the impression for attaching adjoining base brackets with fastener contained within the impression.

Closed Base Shelf. Base shelves shall be formed of not less than #18 gauge steel into a one-piece construction designed to fit snugly around upright columns and base brackets without need of hardware fasteners. Front height shall be at least 3 inches and sides shall have stiffening flanges. Insert integral back divider/guide within web of frame upright.

Shelf End Bracket. Shelf end brackets shall be designed with a 15 degree sloped front edge and shall be formed of not less than #16 gauge steel and all but the rear edge is to be flanged outward approximately 1/4 inch. Rear edge shall have two crimped hooks at top and a positioning tab at bottom for engaging frame upright slots. Also include cup impression to prevent bracket overlapment when units are shelved. Bracket shall extend at least 6 inches above shelf surface.

Adjustable Integral Back Shelf. All shelves shall support book loads of 40 pounds per square foot without deflection in excess of 3/16 inch. Adjustable shelves of 10 inch nominal depth shall be formed of #19 gauge special alloy steel. Nominal depth of shelf shall be 1 inch greater than actual dimension measured from front of shelf to frame upright. The front edge of the shelf shall be box formed 3/4 inch high to receive a snap-on label holder if required. The rear edge of the shelf shall be upturned approximately 1-1/4 inch, forming a hemmed rail that is capable of receiving a sliding book support. Side of shelf to be flanged for locking into end bracket grips. Each shelf shall be a minimum clearance between end brackets of 35-7/16 inches.

Hinged periodical shelf shall consist of sloping display shelves hinged to storage shelf and base shelf brackets. Display shelves shall be 14 inches high and be hinged in such manner as to provide a clear storage height of 8 inches. Lower edge of display shelf shall have flange and turned up lip to provide a 1-3/8-inches clearance behind lip. Display shelves shall be supplied with rubber tips at top and bottom corners for sound deadening and shall stand without holding when in open position. Affix continuous 1-inch-high label holders to front edge of display lip.

Divider type shelf shall be of not less than #18 gauge steel with front edge box formed 3/4 inch high and with back edge formed upward 5 inches and with plates 6 inches high for each shelf opening unless other quantities or heights are specified.

Sliding reference shelves of #18 gauge special alloy steel shall be attached to the undersides of book shelves where specified and shall extend the same depth as shelf above when fully extended. They shall operate on ball bearing extension slides. These shall be single entry only, as double acting shelves prevent simultaneous use on both sides of a free-standing range.

Transverse top bracing channel shall be of #18 gauge steel measuring at least 1 by 1-3/4 by 96 inches and shall be provided on the ratio of one length to every three units of double-faced bookstack sections.

Finish. Component parts shall be prepared for painting by a multi-stage cleaning and phosphatizing process. Material is then to be finished with a fine baking enamel of a medium gloss, applied by electrostatic method, capable of withstanding severe hammer and bending tests without flaking. Surfaces difficult to cover electrostatically are to be hand sprayed prior to entering baking ovens, allowing uniform and complete paint coverage.

Part II

Post-Occupancy Evaluation

10

Definition and Rationale

Although millions of dollars are spent every year to program, design, and construct new library buildings and additions, it is unusual for anyone involved in the process to step back and systematically examine whether the completed building achieved its goals.

Building planners and library administrators write the library building program in order to communicate needs and objectives to the designers. They also spend much time pouring over the architect's plans and schematics to make sure their intentions are implemented in the design. This is the opportunity to correct mistakes and to make sure that the building will be efficient and logical from both the staff and the users' perspectives.

Although plan evaluation is a critical stage in the planning of library buildings, it is done from paper plans or, on occasion, generalized models. It cannot consider the full range of relationships and overlapping dynamics that take place when the building is no longer a plan but actually exists. Staff and users often defy well-founded expectations. Plan evaluation cannot consider the natural synergism of human needs in a complex organization.

No matter how excellent the architect or how diligent the planners are in evaluating the plans, the true test of the building comes when it is built, occupied, and used. Plan evaluation is abstract and primarily an intellectual exercise; post-occupancy evaluation is concrete and involves the natural complexity of real life. Both types of evaluation make important contributions to the improvement of library buildings.

After construction, library administrators and architects normally go through a new facility to make sure that contractors perform all of their obligations before accepting the building. But this microlevel "punch list" evaluation takes place before occupying the building. Even more importantly, the focus is specific and limited and does not, indeed cannot, consider how the building functions at the service level.

New library buildings can benefit from a macrolevel, service-oriented evaluation. A systematic analysis, or post-occupany evaluation, has been done for years in other types of buildings but only rarely in new library buildings. It is also unusual for anyone to take a formal look at how the building works and then share that information with a broader community.

DEFINITION

Post-occupancy evaluation deals with the physical and social aspects of the building and the relationship between the two. The evaluator or evaluation team gathers information on the appearance, efficiency, and maintenance of the building. But just as importantly, the evaluation must examine the attitudes, feelings, interpretations, and experiences of the people who use or work in the environment (Daish et al., 1982, page 77).

Post-occupancy evaluation is "the examination of the effectiveness of designed environments for human users" (Zimring and Reizenstein, 1982). The methods and procedures for post-occupancy evaluations are varied and flexible. In fact, one definition notes that "post-occupancy evaluation is what post-occupancy evaluators do" (Zimring, 1987, page 270).

Many things—some positive, some negative—contribute to this variation. In the real world, how the evaluators conduct the evaluation depends on what they want out of it, for whom it is being done, whether the study will examine the whole building or only part, whether the interest is in staff efficiency or public use, who the study will gather information from, and many other variables. Methods will also be affected by time, resources, funding, and political issues. Finally, the type of inquiry will be affected by the skill and knowledge of the evaluators.

WHY DO IT?

Evaluation of a new building provides a valuable feedback loop. A detailed, careful examination can help finetune the new building, or it can help others learn from the experience.

The designers and planners cannot anticipate the complete range of uses and patterns of interactions between staff or library users and a complex building. The unexpected nearly always happens and, when it does, adjustments in the facility should be made. Prudent managers will even set aside a portion of the equipment and furnishings budget for this purpose. Assuming that every aspect of the building will turn out exactly as the designers intend is dangerously overconfident.

Evaluation can also help establish accountability for the complex and costly process of putting up a new library. It is a formal, systematic way to get information back to people involved with planning, designing, constructing, and operating library buildings. It tells policy makers, funding authorities, building consultants, architects, builders, and library administrators what they did well and what they could have done better.

A post-occupancy evaluation can be implemented by a single library or groups of libraries. It can be done at the state, regional, or national level as part of the requirements for funding the building programs. Several large public library systems have implemented systematic appraisal of new branches in order to improve subsequent construction projects.

PREVIOUS EVALUATIONS

Evaluations of new buildings have been done for many years and are regularly conducted by many organizations, including AT&T and the U.S. General Services Administration. David Carr has developed a methodology for evaluating cultural institutions such as museums, galleries, botanical gardens, and historic restorations (Carr, 1990).

A number of libraries and library systems around the country began performing evaluations of new buildings in the 1980s. Three systems in the Baltimore-Washington, D.C., area are especially active. The Montgomery County Department of Public Libraries, with offices in Rockville, Maryland, began conducting evaluations of new and renovated buildings in the 1980s. Branches of the Baltimore County Library have also been evaluated since 1986.

The Fairfax County Public Library in Virginia developed a post-occupancy evaluation program when the system planned the addition of three new regional libraries and two smaller community libraries, and the renovation of five other buildings. Post-occupancy evaluation was an efficient way to learn from experience and apply that knowledge to other buildings (Clay and Hlavka, 1987).

Libraries in other parts of the country are also beginning to evaluate buildings. The Hennepin County Library in Minnesota has evaluated new buildings since 1987. The Kern County Library in Bakersfield, California, evaluated the Beale Memorial Library in 1989, two years after completion of the new facility.

BARRIERS TO EVALUATION

Post-occupancy evaluation of libraries is still quite rare, however. Despite having made a great investment—or perhaps because of the large sums expended—funding authorities, policy makers, consultants, architects, and library administrators do not as a rule conduct evaluations of new library buildings or additions. The reasons usually seem to be:

- There is never enough time or money.
- Pressing concerns vie for attention. Administrators must tend to problems neglected during the building project while consultants and architects move on to new projects.
- Administrators dislike the paperwork that inevitably comes with a study of this type.
- The joy of bringing a new building into the world can interfere with a systematic, objective appraisal. Alternatively, "postpartum" exhaustion can deter an evaluation.
- No one wants to risk admitting or being caught in failure, especially with a time consuming and expensive a project like a new building or addition.
- Those involved may feel they lack the skills to conduct the study.
- Just about everyone involved—policy makers, consultants, architects, and administrators—feels "It's not my job."

AVAILABLE TOOLS

The guidelines outlined here suggest a series of specific steps that a library administrator can take to evaluate a library building after it has been used for a period of time. They take a pragmatic, action-oriented approach so that librarians involved in the building process can lead or conduct a systematic examination of the new library. They are made with the assumption that the best post-occupancy evaluations "belong" to the people in the organization and that evaluation programs can and ought to become a normal part of the process that follows the planning, design, and construction of a new library building.

The methods are probably familiar to most librarians. In recent years, libraries have increasingly relied on standard planning and evaluation tools. The procedures and tactics recommended in these manuals and guides are also valuable in post-occupancy evaluations. The methods and procedures for the post-occupancy evaluation will draw upon:

> *Output Measures for Public Libraries* (Nancy Van House, et al.). The methods here share a common philosophical tradition that libraries and library services should be evaluated on the basis of performance and the service they provide.

> *Planning and Role Setting for Public Libraries* (Charles McClure, et al.). The framework for the evaluation will also be familiar to many public librarians since it draws much of its structure from this planning manual.

Standard Social Science Methodologies. The procedures for conducting a post-occupancy evaluation draw on those data-gathering methods widely used in the social sciences, including questionnaires, interviews, observation, and a variety of unobtrusive techniques.

The post-occupancy evaluation is similar to conventional library research and many user studies, but there are key differences:

Purpose. Although some post-occupancy evaluations may contribute to a theoretical base, the evaluations are primarily practical and action oriented.

Time. The evaluation takes place after construction of a new building or addition. This should be at least twelve months after opening so that obvious glitches are corrected and users have an opportunity to make accurate and useful appraisals.

Focus. It examines the impact of a new building. The primary emphasis is on the role of the physical environment and its impact on library services and use.

Evaluation. It makes *judgments* about the performance, efficiency, and effectiveness of the building. Description is not enough.

TYPES OF EVALUATION

There are two general reasons for a library to conduct a post-occupancy evaluation. The evaluation can aim at improving and refining the new building or it can examine the bottom line, the final effectiveness of the facility, and the reasons it succeeded or failed. These two types of studies are known as "formative" and "summative" evaluations.

Formative Evaluations. A formative study strives to identify ways to modify and improve the newly opened building. These are not necessarily structural or expensive. Fine-tuning furnishings, adding or changing signs, or making shifts in staff could make the library operate better. Few things perform exactly the way we expect them to and a systematic appraisal can help guide adjustments. They can be useful for three purposes:

1. To refine and modify the physical plant and furnishings.
2. To collect management information in order to reallocate staff and facilities and to better serve the community using the new building.
3. To justify additional funding for these adjustments and modifications.

Summative Evaluations. A post-occupancy evaluation can allow for greater accountability at all levels of the design and construction process. Motivation could include an interest in pure research and furthering the body of library science literature. More often, this evaluation is required by funding authorities or policy makers in the library system or state government in order to advance managerial responsibility or to guarantee good value on their investment. They can be useful for three primary purposes:

- To learn from experience so that managers do not repeat mistakes in subsequent building projects.
- To assist other libraries planning new buildings.
- To justify past investments in the new building by funding authorities.

There are methodological differences between the two approaches. Formative evaluations usually rely heavily on local staff to collect data and conduct analysis. Data-gathering methods tend to be qualitative rather than quantitative. Interviews and participant observation are common. Summative evaluations are usually lead by evaluators from outside the library and the methods tend to be quantitative rather than qualitative. This more hard-nosed approach may emphasize statistical analysis, spatial ratios, cost factors, and usage per square foot.

Most post-occupancy evaluations have both formative and summative components. Their purpose is to improve the library and examine the final impact of the new environment. A formal, systematic examination of the new or renovated facility can make the library a better place and can help others learn from the experience.

11

Getting Ready

Thorough preparation is the difference between successful evaluations and chaos. Weak post-occupancy evaluations usually lack focus, do not have a clear purpose or objectives, and use haphazardly prepared instruments. The key to success in evaluating a library building is good spadework and planning.

SEQUENCE OF STEPS

There is a normal progression in a library post-occupancy evaluation. The sequence leads from planning, to development of methods, to data collection and dissemination. Even within each stage, the evaluators can learn from the previous step. For example, the evaluators might elect to use focus groups early in the study in order to learn about the conceptual orientation of staff and library users. Information gathered here could be used to develop questionnaires or to help direct the inquiry of the expert evaluators later on. The study, then, is refined and focused to respond to what was learned in those first steps.

The sequence of steps in the evaluation is not rigid. Each stage somewhat overlaps one or more stages. An objective might be obvious even before preliminary data collection begins because the objective is evident in the charge. The evaluation team would normally determine some objectives and begin establishing questions to be answered by the study early in the planning stage.

On the other hand, an interview with a staff member halfway into the evaluation could suggest a major question that the team should examine more closely. Even dissemination of findings, normally the final step, should be preceded by interim reports and preliminary discussion of findings. The evaluation team should be prepared to modify the sequencing and allow elements of the evaluation design to emerge as the study progresses.

FIRST ACTIONS

Before the evaluation can get off the ground, those planning the study must examine why it is to be conducted, gain the aid of key figures, determine limitations or constraints, and decide how much effort will be expended.

Clarify the Purpose. The evaluator should first examine why the study will be conducted. Long before establishing specific objectives, the evaluation must consider the reasons and motives for the study. For example, is the intent to improve the library's functions or to share success with others? Will the study be formative, summative, or a combination?

Gain Support and Endorsement. The evaluation team must realize that there will be people who can support or sabotage the post-occupancy evaluation. The success of the study depends on understanding their needs and gaining their cooperation. In many cases, evaluators will need a letter of endorsement in order to gain assistance or even to interview the staff. Gaining support is not a one shot affair. The evaluators must develop and maintain confidence in the evaluation throughout the process. Doubtful or weakening support can affect candidness and access to sources of information. It is especially important to make sure that the library employees understand that the building, not the staff's performance, is the subject of the evaluation.

Determine Limitations or Constraints. Resources, including time and money, are not unlimited. What can you realistically expect to achieve? What personnel and skills are available for the evaluator to draw upon? What limitations could or will be imposed by funding authorities or policy makers? Post-occupancy evaluations are often deeply involved in political issues. Potential restraints or liabilities must be considered and appraised early in the planning process.

Determine Levels of Effort. This determination derives at least in part from the limitations and constraints. There is a continuum ranging from simple, local, and inexpensive efforts to lengthy, sophisticated evaluations that use experts, such as architects and other design consultants, and technical measurement of physical facilities. A basic level of effort uses largely informal or unobtrusive methods and gathers information from readily available sources, such as circulation statistics, turnstyle count, and so forth. Staff may be interviewed but there may be no attempt to survey the broader community. This level of effort in a post-occupancy evaluation might be done by one person in a short period of time with limited finances. A moderate level of effort includes more unobtrusive statistical information such as output and performance measures. Other possible methods include behavior mapping. There is more in-depth interviewing and use of questionnaires than at the basic level. For an extensive level of effort methodologies could include surveying, interviews, and focus groups. Data can be gathered from staff, library users, nonusers, policy makers, designers, and others. Team leaders could bring in architects and library consultants for their expert evaluations. Some studies have included objective measurement of ambient and task lighting, glare levels, noise, temperature, and humidity at work stations and public areas.

LOGISTICS

In determining the level of effort, the evaluators must consider personnel, available expertise, resources, timing, and costs. Logistics are the nagging details evaluators must attend to in order to do the evaluation. They involve physical resources, people, and timing. Questions relating to logistics should be addressed throughout the process of planning the post-occupancy evaluation. It is also beneficial to allow considerable flexibility in logistics. Issues involved include:

Define Responsibilities and Establish Committees. Post-occupancy evaluation works best when there is a team with a variety of skills and perspectives. The evaluation planners must identify the right people and then establish policies and coordinate procedures to ensure that everyone works together. Building evaluations can and should be done in-house, depending on the scope and focus of the study. Daish and his coauthors note that the post-occupancy evaluation must "belong" to as many of the building's personnel as possible. Action-based research of this kind should use as trainers outsiders whose involvement is reduced as the study progresses (Daish et al., 1983, page 55).

It may be useful to bring in outside help in order to:

- Provide subject expertise. Evaluation of mechanical systems or elements of the design may require an outside expert.
- Provide methodological expertise. Local personnel may not have a full range of skills in selecting evaluation goals, developing instruments, or collecting data. In those cases, a consultant could help guide the study and train the staff.
- Avoid bias or the perception of bias. Library personnel sometimes need assistance maintaining an impartial, objective evaluation. More commonly, however, external consultants are necessary to lend the study increased credibility with the library's policy makers or funding authorities.

Allocate Resources. A post-occupancy evaluation can range from a one-day walk-through to a multiyear, multisite study. Cost effectiveness should be considered in the design of the study. For example, while individual interviews might be useful in gathering frank opinions, many evaluators use group interviews with two to ten people in order to hold costs in line (Zimring, 1987, page 288).

Costs. Although post-occupancy evaluations can be conducted inexpensively, the cost of duplicating survey instruments, postage, honoraria for experts (including architects), and other expenses must be addressed. Other resources, such as team access to computers and support staff, must also be considered early in the planning process.

Zimring (1987) developed several formulas to determine the cost of a post-occupancy evaluation. Costs have run .25 to 1.25 percent of the cost of construction or 5 to 8 percent of the design fee. The price of the post-occupancy evaluation of a $2 million building might total $5,000 to $25,000 or even higher.

Because the cost of a post-occupancy evaluation can be more than many libraries are able to easily appropriate, some observers have suggested that funding for evaluations be built into the construction budget right from the start. A small percentage, perhaps around one percent, could be allocated for the post-occupancy evaluation just as many organizations allocate a percentage for public art. The funding authority might suggest or even mandate this allocation.

Timing. Scheduling is also important. A quality evaluation depends on adequate time to do the job well. The evaluation team should have the ability to respond to new leads and unexpected openings that turn up in the data collection process.

PRELIMINARY DATA COLLECTION: LOOKING AROUND

In order to plan a post-occupancy evaluation, the researcher must learn where to look. The clues will come from walking around, talking informally with those involved with the library, and reading key documents, memos, and correspondence. This preliminary investigation provides the substance for selecting evaluation objectives and questions to be answered by the study.

The evaluator should conduct a library "walk-around" in order to get a sense of the library's context and operation. The walk-around is also an excellent way to find out where the potential problems are and to identify areas to investigate further. The walk should also include the neighborhood or the immediate area. The setting includes cultural and social elements, topographic factors (is it flat or hilly), surrounding land use, and architectural styles in the area. Many of these factors, such as terrain, parking, and transportation problems, can significantly affect services offered by the library.

Brief introductory interviews are also useful in this reconnaissance phase. Talking to policy makers and key personnel at funding agencies will provide background information relevant to the personnel and antecedents of the building project. Understanding what went before can shed light on why things are the way they are in the present building.

Building consultants and architects can tell the evaluators their intentions and rationale for various decisions. Administrators and department heads can relate the history of the facility leading up to construction, indicate potential trouble spots that the researcher may want to focus on, or suggest questions that need to be answered.

This first contact will help lead the evaluators to any obvious problems. It can help identify the community and user needs now served by the new facility. Most importantly, it will help the evaluators to plan the study and decide what additional information they will need to gather.

OBJECTIVES

The researchers should generate and screen potential objectives for the evaluation project. Objectives are important because they bring focus to the study and relate directly to the data-collecting methods. The objectives must be action-oriented, measurable, and achievable. Examples might include:

- To determine changes in the quantity of information services provided to the public since the building opened.
- To determine the attitude of library users and community leaders toward the architectural design.
- To enumerate changes in staff productivity since moving into the new building.
- To describe the movement of library users from the entrance to the major service areas in the new building.

Objectives for the post-occupancy evaluation can be relatively broad or quite specific and can come from different sources. Objectives might come from:

- The role and mission statements of the library.
- The objectives of the building program.
- Concerns of the staff about some aspect of the building.
- Outside influences, such as funding authorities that require the evaluation.

Basic documents, such as mission statements and stated library objectives, are good places to start. For example, a public library that sees its primary role as a popular library must examine the physical facility in that light.

Perhaps the greatest source of objectives for the post-occupancy evaluation will come from the objectives for the building spelled out in the building program. For example, the program may have sought to improve access to audio-visual materials or expand the number of seats in quiet study areas. Evaluation goals should seek to learn how successful the planners and designers were in meeting those objectives and whether or not the greater access and expansion has been useful to library patrons. The post-occupancy evaluation can be, if it is made so, an evaluation of the validity of the original planning objectives as well as their effective realization.

Design objectives were used as the basis of the post-occupancy evaluation of a federal building in Ann Arbor, Michigan. These effective objectives were not complex or extremely detailed. In that study, the evaluation examined "(1) relationships between the building and the community; (2) transportation and parking; (3) people's assessment of the building and their work environment; and (4) the relationship between the work environment and worker performance" (Marans and Spreckelmeyer, 1981, page 52).

An objective might be inspired by staff concern for a possible change in library user behavior. For example, library personnel may know that many users are unable to find bound periodicals. The evaluation could specifically examine users' appraisal of the signage system. A secondary goal or implication of the evaluation might be to identify ways to improve any difficiencies identified in the study.

Not all objectives are overt and above board. Hidden agendas can sometimes influence the selection of evaluation objectives or, for that matter, methodologies and collection of data. For example, evaluations may be commissioned in order to promote and advertise the success of one or more members of the building design team. Other times, evaluators are expected to provide condemning documentation for use in a personal vendetta. The unstated objective may be simply to shift blame from one group to another. Needless to say, those who commission the post-occupancy evaluation would be severely disappointed if the report did not conform to their expectations.

The evaluation team must decide how it will deal with hidden agendas once it detects them. Maintaining professional integrity may be difficult, especially when challenged with internal or formative evaluations. Carol Weiss presented an excellent discussion of these issues in her book *Evaluation Research: Methods of Assessing Program Effectiveness* (Weiss, 1972, page 11–13).

Objectives often suggest a comparison of values. For example, the evaluation could compare circulation or other output measures before and after the opening of the new or renovated facility. Qualitative data, such as attitudes and opinions about the building or services, can also be compared before and after the move. In this instance, four objectives could be stated:

1. To compare output measures statistics between the previous and current facilities.
2. To compare cataloging productivity statistics between the previous and current facilities.
3. To compare processing productivity between the previous and current facilities.
4. To compare user attitudes toward the library since occupying the current facility.

Of course, comparable data must be available for this kind of comparison to be valid. The objectives could be diagrammed in order to better understand the research design:

	Old Building	New Building
Circulation		
Cataloging Productivity		
Processing Productivity		
User Attitudes		

It may be useful to relate one set of variables to another. For example, the first objective of a newly expanded library may be to describe the attitudes of staff personnel and library users toward different areas of the library, and a second objective may be to evaluate the lighting levels in staff and public areas. The third objective could be to relate these two variables:

	Ambient Lighting	Natural Lighting	Task Lighting
Staff Attitudes			
User Attitudes			

A statement of objectives can limit or bring definition to the study. Focus can be found by considering the purpose, limitations, constraints and other contextual factors. These include the various phases of the design and construction process that might be examined, the potential for differing perspectives, and the study's scale.

Perspectives. Aspects of the planning, design, and construction processes can be evaluated. The post-occupancy evaluation could target the consultant's contribution and the building program. It might also have as its objective an appraisal of the architect's design or the quality of construction. It could also look at the administrative role in the space management. These perspectives reflect various points of view. Even the perspective of the building's users can be subdivided into two categories: the library patrons and staff.

Most post-occupancy evaluations consider both of these two major perspectives, although any given study might emphasize one or the other. At the same time, an evaluation that emphasizes one perspective will often use the other as an information source. For example, a post-occupancy evaluation with a goal of focusing on the patron's perspective will likely draw a great deal of useful data from staff experience with the library's patrons.

Scale. The scale of the evaluation should also be reflected in evaluation objectives. A library with a new wing might choose to evaluate only that wing or only a public function most directly affected, such as reference services. This narrowing should be considered carefully, however, since a change in one part of a building can significantly affect usage and traffic patterns in other parts of the library.

QUESTIONS

Objectives in applied research lead to questions. The researchers must determine and specify the particular target or piece of information that will be gathered to satisfy each objective. These are not questions on surveys or interviews but questions that the evaluators must answer in their data gathering. For example, a post-occupancy evaluation might have an objective to compare the efficiency of technical services before and after the move to the new facility. Questions that may help the evaluation team meet that objective could include:

- How many print items are cataloged each month?
- How many audio-visual items are cataloged each month?
- How many staff hours are worked each month?
- How long does it take to get an item on the shelf?

A FINAL NOTE ON PLANNING

Good post-occupancy evaluations are well planned. At the same time, however, too rigid a plan can put the evaluators and the evaluation into a straight jacket. The very best plan is one that can remain open and responsive to changing conditions. A chance remark by a staff member during an interview may provide a key to any area that should be followed up, even if it means revising the plan. A framework that incorporates a heuristic or self-adjusting mechanism is able to respond and use that new information (Zimring, 1987, pages 275–75).

This flexibility also helps the library's personnel become more deeply involved and committed to the evaluation process. As Daish wrote, post-occupancy evaluation "is a learning process. It must be open and flexible to allow all those concerned to obtain both personal and corporate benefits. By supporting the idea of having a programme which belongs to and benefits those concerned, many of the barriers to post-occupancy evaluation can be lowered" (Daish et al., 1983, page 55).

12

Sources, Analysis, and Design

Designing an evaluation requires a great deal of planning. Beyond formulating objectives and questions, the evaluators need to chart out where the information will come from, how it will be gathered and analyzed, and how judgments will be made.

SOURCES OF INFORMATION

Perhaps the best way to find out how the building works and relates to users is either to ask the people involved or to watch them using the building. Users of the building are central to the evaluation. Even the mechanical aspects must be interpreted and filtered through human perceptions. A post-occupancy evaluation might center on energy conservation or the heating, ventilation, and air conditioning system, for example. But even a study directed at nonhuman aspects of the building requires a well-grounded understanding of how people actually use the library.

Key sources include the staff, library users, outside experts, and a range of others who are either involved or interested in the library building.

Staff. The people who work in the library will probably prove to be the richest source of information about the building. They can tell the evaluators how the building affects staff efficiency but they can also provide valuable data on how well library users relate to the building.

All employees should be brought into the evaluation. Evaluators should keep in mind that while the professional and administrative staff will have a great deal to contribute, the support staff usually outnumbers librarians two to one and often has a great deal of direct contact with users. Maintenance and custodial personnel are especially valuable sources of information and should play a major role.

Marans and Spreckelmeyer warned that evaluation by staff members will likely be influenced by what they see the most, and that their attitude toward the entire building is often affected by where they work: "People's feelings about their agencies were to a large extent influenced by their views about the immediate work environment" (1981, page 112). Furthermore, staff perceptions of the work place are affected by a complex of psychological and social factors which are a part of the dynamics of the whole organization. This aspect of staff appraisal is discussed in the section "Comparison Standards" later in this chapter.

Users. There are different kinds of users, and evaluators will have to decide which users to target and how they will gather information from each. Users can be distinguished by a range of demographic characteristics: age, geographic location, income, ethnic background, and so forth. The decision to target specific user groups will depend on the community and the goals of the post-occupancy evaluation.

Evaluation design and methodologies are affected by these decisions. The sample could be stratified (20 percent senior citizens, 20 percent business people, 40 percent undifferentiated adults, 20 percent children, for example) rather than completely random. Data-collecting methods will also be affected. Adults may respond to a mailed questionnaire but children might respond better to an interview the library. Other groups and nonusers may require special strategies.

The evaluations offered will depend on personal objectives and the purpose for using the library: "The specificity of experience of a place is a reflection of the degree to which the place contributes to objectives a person might have" (Canter, 1983, page 667). That is, if a user's purpose is to spend a quiet hour reflecting on Cicero or to grab a snooze in the "cathedral of learning," his or her appraisal of a modern library with a range of electronic services and noisy programs will not be favorable.

Experts. Independent appraisals by authoritative and knowledgeable outsiders can provide a unique and valuable perspective. However, several observers have noted that, on occasion, the buildings experts like best are disliked by the people who use or work in them.

The outside experts should be a central part of the evaluation team, not isolated from the objectives or methods of the study. The evaluation director must guide them and provide information and logistical resources. Lack of communication of objectives, purposes, and appropriate perspectives could result in unwanted redundencies or incomplete reports.

Outside experts cannot be expected to understand requirements that other team members take for granted because of their longer involvement with the study. For example, evaluation directors should discuss the kinds of things they are looking for and strategies for collecting the information. A director may recommend that the experts evaluate from the perspective of user efficiency or staff productivity, depending on the needs of each evaluation. Specific suggestions and ways that the experts might organize their evaluations are outlined in Chapter 14.

Other Stakeholders. Community leaders, political figures, funding and policy authorities, library consultants, contractors, the architectural team, and others involved in the project can help the evaluation team understand the prehistory and rationale of the design.

ANALYSIS

The evaluators should determine how specific information will be used and analyzed once it is collected. There is a natural tendency to ask unnecessary questions or questions that shed little light. Simple curiosity is not enough; questions should be asked in order to collect specific information. Unnecessarily long instruments waste the time of both respondents and the researchers.

The format of questions sometimes leads to useless data. If it is difficult or impossible to summarize or code responses, the data cannot be used effectively. If the evaluators are not sure how a question will be used, it should be dropped from the questionnaire or interview. Careful pruning should take place before collecting the information.

Information can be analyzed in many different ways, and those options should be considered while the evaluation is being planned. For example, if the collected data will be broken down by the demographic characteristics of the different library users (age, section of town, gender, and so forth), then the instruments should be designed with that in mind. Conversely, if the evaluators do not plan to analyze the study with respect to these characteristics, there is no need to ask questions related to them. Variation in use of the building during different times of the day, days of the week, or seasons of the year may be factors in the analysis.

Other factors, such as various material formats, subject areas, or special collections should be considered in planning the design of instruments.

STANDARDS

Building description is not enough in post-occupancy evaluation. Judgments must be made. The word evaluation contains the concept of value and the analysis must include judgments about the value of the building.

Standards are the bases for comparison used in the evaluation. The evaluators must plan how they are going to come to conclusions about the suitability and efficiency of the building. What is good and bad design? How can the evaluators recognize an effective or ineffective building? How will they decide physical and aesthetic questions? What will be the basis for judgment? How will the evaluators know value when they see it? Questions of standards should also be addressed at the time the evaluators plan the analysis.

There are many different types of standards: formal, informal, even unarticulated standards. The standards considered here are comparison standards, goal-based standards, expert standards, and formal standards.

Comparison Standards. The public, staff, and others often compare the new library to the old facility. Unfortunately, they sometimes compare the new, modern building to their memories of the building they used as children. The basis of comparison becomes what they know or what they had before. Even though this informal standard is often not articulated, it can be very important.

Comparison standards can be more formal and specifc when different performance measures are compared. How, for example, do the output measures compare pre- and post-occupancy? Circulation, number of reference questions asked, and attendance at programs before occupancy can be the basis for judgment. Subjective data can also be used for comparison.

The staff's standard of comparison can become more sophisticated. Not only are they likely to compare the new work environment to other libraries or what they had before, but they might also evaluate on the basis of what their colleagues and peers in the building have (better view, closer to the boss or the shelf list, and so forth) or their aspirations and expectations. As Marans and Spreckelmeyer point out, the staff's evaluation of the work environment reflects physical attributes but also psychological and organizational components (1981, page 111).

Parking can illustrate this point. How the staff evaluates the parking in the new facility will likely reflect more than the simple availability of parking spaces but also the amount of parking availability before opening the new facility and any charges. If parking was free at the old library, any charge at the new facility will draw considerable condemnation. Staff appraisal of the parking facility could reflect the availability of dedicated, marked spaces for administrators and the staff's perception of how fairly those spaces are allocated. Moreover, one or two negative experiences with something as peripheral as parking can influence the general evaluation of the whole building.

There is a large subjective component in the standards of both users and staff. Evaluators must remember that the appraisal of the building offered by staff and library users is not solely dependent on the actual attributes of the building: "the individual's perception and assessment of a particular environmental attribute is dependent on two factors: the standards against which he or she judges that attribute and the objective attribute itself" (Marans and Spreckelmeyer, 1981, page 25). For this reason, it is often valuable to impose other standards and bring in outside experts to provide another, perhaps more objective, perspective.

Goal-based Standards. This could be considered a type of comparison standard since it compares expectations or objectives with actual performance. The standards are the objectives established by planners, designers, and builders when they set out to plan and construct the building.

Expert Standards. These standards could be established by an architectural jury or a librarian with experience in library planning who tours and appraises the building. Published recommendations could be used for comparison. Normal spatial proportions and ratios (the recommended area for each workstation or the usual percentage of unassigned areas), costs for comparable buildings, number of parking spaces, seating, bookstacks and so forth can be used as a standard. The American Library Association's Checklist of Library Building Design Considerations could be used to guide the evaluation of key functions and services.

A demonstration program funded by the Connecticut State Library in 1989 provided money for an expert evaluation component in a postoccupancy evaluation. Two experts contributed to this study. The architect concentrated on aesthetic and architectural design elements of the building. The library expert examined building design from a functional point of view. Written reports are included in Chapter 15 of this document. In the future, the Connecticut Library Association will nominate a librarian with experience in library planning, while the Connecticut Chapter of the American Institute of Architects will select an architect with experience in library design to participate in these demonstration evaluations.

Formal Standards. These standards might be based on criteria developed by governmental agencies or professional associations. Formal standards might enumerate the number of seats required, square footage in different areas, or other characteristics. Since the standards of governmental agencies usually carry a mandate of compliance, they are usually lower than those of professional associations which are actually, as a rule, guidelines.

STATISTICS

Excellent studies can be conducted with limited statistical expertise. Usually no hypotheses are tested and, since the purpose is to evaluate a single library, there is little need to generalize the results to a larger population. Purposive sampling, where the evaluator selects particular users to interview, could be as useful as random sampling. The statistics employed in post-occupancy evaluations will often reflect this narrowed focus.

Statistics should help evaluators and others understand the library building and how it functions: "In all cases, clarity is preferable to quasi-scientific mystification" (Zimring, 1987, page 281). Statistics may provide "background music" for the study but should not be allowed to get in the way of the evaluation or judgment about the building's usefulness.

Most studies of this type require only basic descriptive statistics, such as averages and median values. If the evaluators are so inclined and have the skills, more sophisticated statistical analyses could be used. Simple correlation could be especially useful, and inferential statistics, such as Chi Square, could contribute to understanding. Occasionally, more high-powered statistical procedures are used. One major, sixteen-month long evaluation of a federal office building used bivariate and multivariate analysis in order to reduce and summarize a large amount of data. Regression analysis was used to determine which of forty-seven factors contributed to employee satisfaction or dissatisfaction with the building (Marans and Spreckelmeyer, 1981, page 106).

SAMPLING

Many librarians rely on volunteer samples for interviews or question-naires. It may appear easier, faster, and cheaper to pass out questionnaires to users as they enter the building or to leave a stack of questionnaires at the circulation desk. The value of information collected this way, however, is questionable.

People who volunteer to fill out a survey are not typical of most community residents or library users. They have more time than most and tend to be more favorably disposed to the library. Volunteer samples may be a good way to collect praise and glad tidings for the library, but they usually contribute little to our understanding of problems or solutions.

The sample does not have to be very large. Information from a hundred randomly selected respondents may be preferable to a thousand responses from library users who voluntarily picked up and filled out their questionnaires. For example, evaluators in Ann Arbor, Michigan, interviewed by telephone a randomly selected sample of 113 local residents out of the total city population of over 107,000. This sixteen month post-occupancy evaluation of a federal building also collected data from a sample of people entering and leaving the building and from those working in the facility (Marans and Spreckelmeyer, 1981, page 15).

Drawing a sample is not difficult and libraries can often find people who will assist in the process. Often a computer running the library's circulation system can be used to randomly select a sample from the list of library users. Libraries with manual circulation systems can select a sample by using a list of random numbers printed in the back of many statistics textbooks. The specific steps for selecting a sample can be found in most research methods textbooks.

Although purposive sampling, or intentionally interviewing specific people from particular groups, is often good practice, normal procedures designed to achieve a degree of rigor, such as random or stratified sampling, should be used whenever feasible.

CREATING INSTRUMENTS

Questionnaires, interview schedules, checklists diary formats, and observation forms need instruments or documents to gather information for post-occupancy evaluations. The evaluation team will usually need different versions of an instrument for staff, adult users, children, or others.

Developing instruments should take place late in the planning process. Many times evaluators jump too quickly into methodological procedures and begin drafting questionnaires before adequately considering objectives, logistics, types of analysis and other important elements of the research design.

The usual procedures for creating an instrument include:

Identify Evaluator Questions. These questions are not the specific items appearing on a survey but rather the information the evaluators need in order to meet the evaluation objectives. Questions relate to what the evaluators need to know. They are derived from goals and objectives, the library walk-around, reviews of documents, and preliminary discussion with staff, users, and others. After information needs are identified, appropriate methodologies (questionnaires, interviews, observation, and so forth) can be selected.

Select Methodologies. A combination of methods usually provides the perspective and corroborative support needed for a good evaluation. Methods often used in post-occupancy evaluations are outlined in Chapter 13.

Draft the Instrument. Previous post-occupancy evaluations might yield examples of questions or even complete instruments which can be used in the present study. Instruments created specifically can be drafted by several members of the team in order to gain the widest perspective.

Review Drafts and Pretest. This stage is often side-stepped in the mistaken belief that the evaluators can save time or money. After letting the draft version season for a day or two, the evaluators should re-examine the instrument and then ask colleagues or other evaluators to criticize it. Several revisions may be necessary.

After reworking the draft, the evaluation team should test the instrument in a library not involved with the post-occupancy evaluation. Those examining the instrument should be asked to look for possible sources of confusion, ambiguity, or other trouble spots.

Revise the Instrument. Peer review and pretesting will produce a better instrument. The evaluators should take care to keep the instrument as clean and simple as possible. There is a natural tendency for instruments to grow in length and complexity as time passes and they are handled by more people. Team members should always ask themselves how the instrument could be made shorter and clearer.

13

Methodologies

The methods presented here are options or tools in the evaluator's tool chest. Specific choices will depend on the purpose, objectives, and scope of the post-occupancy evaluation. For example, a library that seeks to reallocate staff and justify additional funding could emphasize formative internal, quantitative methods. Another library might hope to justify an earlier allocation from an outside funding source by emphasizing a summative approach which relies on expert judgments and comparative data from other building projects.

The scope of the study can also influence the methodologies used. A library might select only specific aspects of a building or an addition for its post-occupancy evaluation. If an objective is to determine why some seats or parts of the library are not used, the method known as behavioral mapping could provide useful data. If an objective is to determine the effect of the new building on community support, then a focus group might be the best choice. If an objective is to determine the effect of the new facility on staff efficiency, then diaries and time-motion studies could produce answers.

Generally, the best strategy is a combination of methodologies. A questionnaire administered to the staff, for example, could provide a slant that the expert observation did not reveal. This triangulation, or gaining of perspective from different vantage points, often results in the strongest study. Multiple methods can also strengthen the study by corroborating evidence or suggesting areas for detailed examination.

METHODOLOGIES

The full range of methods and techniques for gathering information used in the social sciences might be used in post-occupancy evaluation. The available repertoire is extensive. Over a decade ago, an analysis by Bechtel and Srivastava (1978) found that at least fourteen data-gathering methods had been used in post-occupancy evaluations:

- Open-ended interviews
- Closed-ended interviews
- Cognitive maps
- Behavioral maps
- Diaries
- Direct observation
- Participant observation

- Time-lapse photography
- Motion picture photography
- Questionnaires
- Psychological tests
- Adjective checklists
- Archival data
- Demographic data

Since then, many other methods, including focus groups and walk-through interviews, have been used in post-occupancy evaluations.

OBTRUSIVE MEASURES

Evaluation methods can be categorized as obtrusive and unobtrusive. Any procedures that require the active participation of users, staff, or others, such as questionnaires and interviews, are considered obtrusive measures. Obtrusive methods assume respondents have information or opinions to provide and are willing and able to share that information. Many respondents, however, may not be good sources of information, and the evaluation team should consider whether accurate information might better be gathered by unobtrusive measures, such as observing users or analyzing performance measures. The evaluators might also consider using some unobtrusive measures to confirm the data gathered by questionnaires and interviews.

Information gathered by obtrusive measures can be subjective and nonquantitative, objective and quantitative, or a combination. The evaluators could use questionnaires to ask about staff perceptions or attitudes towards the heating system or other aspects of the building. The same methodology could also gather objective data on, for example, the number of times an employee uses the staff lounge or the number of times maintenance problems are encountered.

Questionnaire Surveys. Questionnaires are excellent ways to get information cheaply and efficiently from large numbers of people. They can be used for staff, users, and others. They are best for collecting objective data or explaining motivations; they are less effective at gathering information on feelings and emotions (Zimring, 1987, page 277).

Questionnaires and interviews can vary by the amount of control and structure imposed on responses. Highly structured instruments have closed-ended formats that ask the respondents to check off appropriate answers. Less structured instruments have an open-ended format that allows the respondents to answer in their own words and with less prompting (and, therefore, less potential bias) from the researchers.

Closed-ended formats get more responses because they are easy to fill out. They also produce information that is easier to analyze. Open-ended formats are better when the evaluators want to hear staff or users describe attitudes or how they use the building in their own words. The less structured format is also preferred in early or exploratory data gathering.

The best questionnaires are brief, well thoughtout, and physically attractive. They must have adequate white space and the evaluators must give attention to typography and page design. The arrangement and flow of questions must be logical. Every question should be there for a specific reason.

The selected sample should be given first class treatment. They should get good quality letters addressed by name. Cover letters should explain the importance and relevance of the study. Endorsement by an authority or sanctioning group, follow-up letters, and even telephone calls should be used to pursue those who do not respond.

Interviews. The merits of structured and unstructured questionnaire formats also apply to interview instruments or schedules. Open-ended questions in interviews are especially important for getting respondents to reveal what is significant to them. Sometimes the evaluator will have a general map of the discussion but allow the respondent to answer in his or her own words without having to respond to questions in a specific sequence (Zimring, 1987, page 287).

Interviews are more expensive and take longer to conduct than questionnaires, but some people who would refuse to fill out a questionnaire will participate in an interview. Also, some library users, such as young children, may not be able to handle a questionnaire.

Walk-through Interviews. This methodology was used successfully in several post-occupancy evaluations conducted in New Zealand. It is a very efficient way to gather a great deal of information from many people, especially staff. It emphasizes the building users or occupants and helps the staff connect with the post-occupancy evaluation (Daish et al., 1982; Zimring, 1987, pages 285–86).

In this methodology, an evaluation team walks through the building and interviews staff and others in their normal work place. The primary advantage is that references to specific aspects of the building are made in the environment, and the evaluator's understanding of comments can be clarified and reinforced by talking about those aspects of the facility.

Most walk-through interviews take place with groups of no larger than twelve to fourteen people. Evaluators give a brief (thirty-minute) introduction and explanation of the study and then meet with building occupants in their normal work place for another thirty to sixty minutes. Afterwards, in a debriefing or summary conference, evaluators clarify their perceptions and ask for recommendations. Daish recommends that the data-collecting team choose a designated facilitator and a recorder. The facilitator serves as the team leader or contact, while the recorder takes notes and writes down comments (Daish et al., 1982, page 81).

The interview format is largely unstructured with many open-ended questions. Often the interview schedule responds to leads presented by the work being done, the comments of the staff, or physical aspects of the area. Some potential questions include:

- What happens here?
- What do you think is good about this part of the building?
- What do you think works well?
- What do you think is bad about this part of the building?
- What do you think should be changed?
- What do you think is important about this space?
- How good would you say the lighting is here?

Diaries. This technique can be useful for collecting data from staff. Many different formats have proved successful including precoded checklists, use cards on which staff movements and traffic patterns are recorded, as well as more conventional journal entries.

Diaries are often used to record only critical incidents. This technique seems to work especially well because participants do not have to write down everything that happens. Instead, they note only very specific and concrete information shortly after it occurs (Zimring, 1987, page 291). Administrators might be asked to record instances of congestion with users or patron complaints. Custodians could record when they encountered a maintenance problem or an equipment breakdown.

Observation. This methodology can be either obtrusive or unobtrusive. Observation techniques can be used by themselves or to supplement or cross-verify reports collected with questionnaires or interviews. They can give researchers an empathetic understanding of an area or the building because the evaluators are exposed to the full range of behaviors, discussions, traffic flow, use of furnishings, and other activities (Zimring, 1987, page 291).

Observation methods can be detailed and specific or impressionistic and exploratory. Impressionistic observations are made early in the library walk-around, as evaluators identify areas for additional research. A good reading of the building early in the inquiry frequently opens up lines of inquiry or suggests questions.

Impressionistic observations might also provide a useful, although subjective, sense of the building and how well it works. Evaluators' reactions to congestion in work areas might support or contrast with the actual square foot area provided personnel or staff members' subjective evaluations of those work rooms. For example, the evaluators appraisal of the work area could help reconcile why staff members feel cramped even though the available square footage exceeds office norms.

Observation can also provide large amounts of objective, quantifiable information. Detailed, objective observations can be recorded on charts or by creating behavioral maps, a technique that uses floor plans and coding schemes to note specific behaviors and the length of time each behavior takes. However, some authorities warn that evaluators can collect very detailed behavior information by observation for only a limited length of time.

Participant observation is the standard research methodology of the ethnographer. The evaluator must get approval from a group (usually staff members and their superiors) to observe what it does and to ask questions about its work as it relates to the building. There is no subterfuge; the evaluator becomes part of the day-to-day work flow and asks questions about procedures and building performance as situations occur.

Participant observation is frequently among the best techniques to gather information on children's use of the library. Getting accurate and useful information from children can be tricky. Just as the ethnographer must avoid cultural bias when studyiing a foreign culture, the adult researcher must recognize that children are cognitively and socially different than adults. Their appraisal of the environment and their ability to report those perceptions put additional obligations on the evaluators.

In observing staff work areas, the evaluation team should go beyond the physical properties of the work areas and examine how the facility ties into the dynamics of the work place. The sociology and psychology of the work place should be considered. Work flow and the movement of materials and people have social as well as physical dimensions. The team will want to consider issues relating to both formal and informal lines of authority and channels of communication in the use of the facility.

It might be a good idea to graphically represent the relationships between the different areas and the normal work flow among them. The test of the evaluation lies in how well the physical facility matches the conceptual work relationships. As shown in this diagram, the arrows represent work areas with primary contacts or shared facilities, equipment, or files:

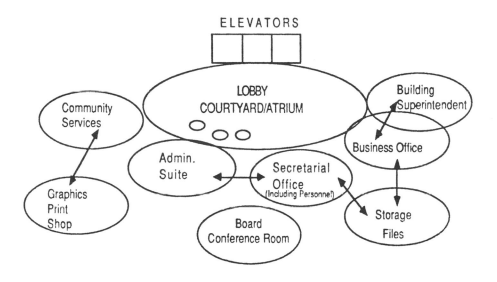

Focus Groups. This methodology is frequently used in marketing research. It can collect a great deal of in-depth information from a very small sample. If questionnaire surveys are sometimes criticized as being a mile wide and an inch deep, focus groups may be said to be an inch wide and a mile deep.

Normally, a trained focus group leader leads a discussion of fourteen to eighteen library users or staff for two to three hours. This technique is especially valuable for gathering information on deeply seated feelings about the library. Because conversations are held in a group setting, discussion often helps participants articulate attitudes and opinions that were previously not well defined. Focus groups might also be used early in the evaluation so that the impressions and attitudes that emerge can be more fully explored in subsequent procedures.

A focus group is not simply a group interview. An unskilled focus group leader will often ask one-dimensional questions (what services do you use?) that might better be gathered by observations, surveys, or by output measures. The alternative methods are less expensive, gather information from a broader sample, and are preferable to a badly led focus group.

A trained and skilled leader, on the other hand, will be able to probe and explore motives. This technique is ideal for answering questions relating to subjective impressions and feelings: How do you feel about the use of large graphics in the children's room? Has your feeling about the community changed since the old library was torn down and the new building constructed?

UNOBTRUSIVE MEASURES

Library research has used this approach at least since publication of *Unobtrusive Measures; Nonreactive Research in the Social Sciences* (Eugene Webb et al., 1966). The basic premise behind the use of unobtrusive measures is that you can learn a great deal about the library and its use by looking at how things wear ("erosion") and the things that are left in the building ("traces").

In recent years, unobtrusive measures have come to be associated with the undercover evaluation of reference service. Webb's definition does not include this kind of intervention but, rather, emphasizes looking at the library or environment for evidence indicating how visitors used the library.

Carpet and furniture wear is an obvious result of patron and staff activity, and this kind of erosion might tell the evaluators something about the type of use. Traces include trash or other evidence of use left around the library. Reference books on tables away from the reference area, for example, may suggest that the administrators might want to more closely examine the reference area's seating, lighting, noise control or other ambient qualities.

"Adaptations for use" can also be useful for telling evaluators about the success or failure of some aspect of the building. Library users make adaptions to make the environment more to their liking. They indicate that the environment probably did not serve its original intentions very well, or that users impose different intentions.

These improvements might include moving furniture around, pushing tables together, or using chairs as hassocks. They suggest that the library might need bigger tables, more lounge chairs or repositioned furnishings. Rather than fighting these adaptations and constantly struggling to reimpose the library's sense of how things should be, the evaluators should see such traces as opportunities to modify and improve the facility.

Documents. Evaluators should examine and summarize pertinent documents, including planning documents, the library building program, schematics, memos, and correspondence. The evaluator can examine these documents to determine background information and motivations (Zimring, 1987, pages 284–85), such as:

- How and why the decision to build was made.
- Who determined building requirements.
- Whether there were any unusual functional requirements.
- Whether the present use of the building is in line with the original plan.
- Whether there is anything unusual about the design, construction, or environment.

Performance Measures. Performance and output measures are especially useful unobtrusive data for post-occupancy evaluations. They are quantitative, reasonably objective, and normally quite easy to collect. Thanks to the work of Ernest DeProspo, Doug Zweizig, Nancy Van House, and many others, performance or output measures are widely used by many libraries. Circulation and library use normally takes a jump immediately after opening a new building. With these methods it is possible to track trends over a number of years and better discern the impact of the building or the expansion over time.

Analysis of output measures might suggest the need to reallocate or reassign staff or to hire additional personnel. For example, a 50 percent increase in reference questions or a doubling of adult nonfiction circulation is convincing evidence for additional staff. In a summative evaluation, output measures can be the key instrument to justify construction expenditures to funding authorities.

Some of the most commonly used output measures include:

- Circulation statistics, including breakdowns by type of user (adult, student, children, and so forth) and type of material (fiction and nonfiction, audio-visual materials, and so forth). If the design emphasizes particular areas or collections (for example, archives, Spanish language, young adult materials) these should be watched to note changes in use patterns.
- In-library use per capita
- Library visits per capita
- Program attendance per capita
- Title, author, subject browsing percentage
- Fill rate
- Reference transactions per capita
- Turnover rate
- Document delivery

Unobtrusive Observation. As noted earlier, observations can be obtrusive or unobtrusive. Unobtrusive observations can be as simple as a preliminary walk-through or as detailed as a month of behavior mapping. They involve minimal interaction with clientele and, as a result, can be made at any time.

Another advantage of observing unobtrusively is that facility users do not have to consciously cooperate with the evaluator. Users, whether patrons or staff, do not have to change their patterns or interrupt their normal activities in order to answer questions. The study is strengthened by reducing one potential source of bias.

Observations should be systematically recorded. Authorities have noted, however, that detailed observation is extremely tiring and should only be done for limited periods. With the exception of preliminary or background observation conducted at the beginning of a study, detailed and extended observation should examine fairly small areas of the building or specific aspects of user behavior. Time sampling (recording observations at selected times) or behavior sampling (waiting for specific behavior to occur) can simplify the observation process.

Carr uses nonquantitative observational techniques to evaluate cultural or educative environments. His approach emphasizes impressionistic, qualitative inquiry. Carr explains that the evaluation must "recognize as data far more than demographic patterns, attendance records, economic profiles and use statistics. If we must count things, perhaps we should start with aspirations, frustrations, and fears. Whatever we count, the most important treasure among our data will be the human voice" (Carr, 1990, page 5). In this naturalistic approach, the observers ask themselves naive questions about the environment: What's going on here? What's all this stuff about? What does it mean to me? What is the conceptual center of this facility? What is the user's problem here? In what ways might human beings think, act, interact, and construct knowledge for themselves here?

Behavior Mapping. Behavior mapping is a systematic technique for recording detailed observations. This methodology notes behavior on a floorpan of the building, identifies the kind and frequency of behavior and demonstrates their association with a design feature. It is usually done on a small scale, such as a room or some other well-defined area of the library.

Three factors—specific behaviors, time, and space (or location in the library)—are combined on a detailed map of the area under examination. The steps for building a behavior map are:

- Create a map or floor plan of the area under study. The map should be detailed and include furnishings and all physical elements. Most maps used in this method have a grid marking each square foot.
- Decide on categories of behavior to be recorded. This is a critical stage because it defines the types and magnitude of behaviors that will be noted by the evaluators. Behaviors might include things like talking, reading, walking, sleeping, and so forth.
- Give each behavior a code or discrete abbreviation.
- Observe the area under study and, using codes, record each behavior and time frame on the map.

This methodology provides use data far beyond circulation statistics or most output measures; it establishes hierarchies of use; it can chart ebbs and flows and movement within the building. It can suggest the need to modify the physical facility or realign staff and provide guidance on how to do it.

14

Substantive Orientation and Conducting the Study

What should the evaluation team look for? Is it enough to simply conduct the evaluation on the basis of the objectives established in the building program or standards established by professional associations? Is it enough to let staff or user perceptions and concerns guide the study? What should the evaluator consider in the library building itself?

The objectives stated in the building program are usually good starting points for deciding whether or not the building measures up to expectations. The objectives provide the evaluation with a target and a standard for judgment. If, for example, an objective of the building program was to increase seating by 40 percent, the evaluators can easily check the number of seats and draw clear, quantifiable conclusions.

The *Checklist of Library Building Design Considerations* (1988) gives evaluators an extensive list of things to look for, although it does not do much to guide evaluators in judging which considerations are more or less valuable to a particular library. Those decisions should be based on the library's mission, roles, and objectives.

The *Checklist* suggests over 324 questions, many with extensive subdivisions, that should be asked concerning the building's facilities. The main sections in the *Checklist* deal with accessibility, bookstacks and shelving, children's facilities, circulation, convenience facilities, equipment, the exterior and interior, future developments, mechanicals and noise control, reference facilities, communication equipment, the environment, security systems, seating, and site.

Library users and the staff will also guide the evaluation team to areas or aspects of the building that require closer scrutiny. Although their insights and experience can be tremendously helpful, sometimes staff and library users can not provide much help in making judgments about how well the building turned out. They often do not have the subject knowledge or breadth of experience to know what is possible or desirable in a building. As noted earlier, their standard of reference may be an antiquated, inefficient building.

Evaluators, especially those with limited experience in library design, need a broader substantive orientation or sense of what is possible, desirable, and good in a library building. There are many excellent books on library design, and anyone planning to evaluate a building should be reasonably well versed in the design principles presented in those works.

While it would certainly not be efficient, and perhaps foolhardy, to reproduce even a part of those documents, a summary of principles and major design concerns could be useful to guide the evaluation.

EXPERT EVALUATION

Outside authorities, such as library planners and architects brought in to provide expertise for the post-occupancy evaluation, can also suggest a different orientation for the study. The evaluation director should allow considerable latitude to the experts in how they go about their work. They should be encouraged to draw on their range of experience, and the structure of the evaluation should not inhibit their expertise or creativity.

However, it may be useful to suggest an array of tools and approaches they may be useful. The *Checklist of Design Considerations* as well as data collected in the early phases of the post-occupancy evaluation should be available to evaluators. This information might include survey results, focus group reports, and statistics on output measures. The experts' evaluations might be organized by personal reactions (what they liked or didn't like), cost or difficulty of adjustment (things that can be easily changed and things that require long-range planning), or physical aspects (exterior and interior architecture).

Two approaches that may be most useful to guide both the experts and the entire post-occupancy evaluation are based on the user's sequence of access and staff productivity.

SEQUENCE OF ACCESS

The relationships among areas and the flow from one part of the library to another is important in the evaluation. However, there are many different sequences of access, each reflecting the different needs and uses of the library. The primary sequence is from finding tools (catalog and indexes) to the actual materials. There are, however, other sequences. The browser's sequence of access will differ, for example, from the subject searcher's.

An excellent way to visualize this sequence or movement of library users is to imagine a patron entering the building. The evaluator should consider the many different uses of the library and how those uses will affect the sequence of access.

Some questions that may be asked include: Is it convenient to enter the library from the parking lot? Is it unnecessarily distant from the entrance? Is the slope from the parking lot to the entrance less than a ten to one incline? Is the entrance clearly visible and inviting?

What will the user see first? Upon entering the building, what features will dominate? Will the user know where to go and how to get what is needed? Is the path open, visible, and logical? Or is it confused and crowded by collections of materials and equipment? Do tall bookstacks or tower display racks block the view of major collections or service areas?

Do the groupings of services orient the user to service relationships? Are the relationships rational and efficient? Are furnishings and seating appropriate to user sequence of access? Are there study carrels, for example, far from noisy staff service areas and the entrance? Are there oversized tables near the newspapers?

STAFF PRODUCTIVITY

Staff efficiency is a particularly important element to consider in the building's design. The major concern is that the staff work areas and the movement of materials is efficient and logical. Hierarchies of use also apply to work areas.

The progression of materials from the library's loading dock to the cataloging and processing area and then to public areas should be natural and simple. It should not be necessary, for example, to repeatedly move people or materials up and down between floors or from one end of the building to the other.

Similarly, the movement of staff should not interfere with productive work. For example, personnel from the reference or audio-visual departments should not have to walk through a staff work area in order to get to the restrooms or staff lounge. Materials, storage areas, and working tools should be located where they will be used. Several local storage areas may be more productive than a single, less accessible central storage area.

Questions that might guide the evaluation include: Are the circulation areas designed for efficient use of current and future systems? Is there room for book trucks in circulation and technical services work areas? Are the work stations large and flexible enough to allow modifications for changing tasks and new technologies?

HIERARCHY OF USE

The evaluators should examine how the facility accommodates different volumes of use. The design should reflect the fact that some materials and different parts of the library get more use than others. Size and spatial proportions should be in line with the use they get. Furthermore, the different areas of the building must be related to each other. Traffic flow and normal progression of use through the building should be a central consideration.

There are two aspects to the hierarchy of use: intensity of use and the length of time used. Some materials or areas, such as circulation, are used by many at a given time but not necessarily for a long period. Other areas, such as quiet study areas, are used by fewer people but for longer periods.

The study should examine the numbers of people in a given area at any one time, and patterns of steady or consistent use of particular furnishings or functions—the so-called "hot seats." The evaluation should consider how the building relates to different use patterns in:

- Reference
- New books
- Current newspapers and magazines
- Bookstacks
- Audio-visual materials
- Older newspapers and magazines
- Special collections and archives
- Children's room (picture books, etc.)
- Study areas
- Lounge areas

In general, those areas with the greatest intensity of use should be located nearest the entrance and near to one another. Circulation, the browsing area, and reference are usually intensively used. Low-intensity areas and those parts of the library used for longer periods of time can be located at a greater distance from the entrance and close to each other. Study areas and areas with back issues of bound periodicals are used for longer periods than others in most libraries.

Types of seating are directly relevant to these issues. The evaluators will want to consider the availability and proportion of stand-up access for short-term use versus long-term lounge seating.

Noise control is another concern that should be reflected in the design. Intensively used areas tend to be noisy and should be shielded or at least distant from quiet reading areas. Traffic creates noise and the route between two high-intensity areas should not be through a low-intensity area. Similarly, the only access to the children's area should not be through the adult reading area. In general, library users should walk through noisy areas to get to quiet areas rather than the other way around.

MACHINE REQUIREMENTS

Libraries and library users are increasingly dependent on technology to store and retrieve information. Evaluators must consider how the design accommodates equipment and the relationship between materials and the machines needed to use them. The evaluation should examine whether the machines are near the area where the materials are stored. Since machines often require ancilliary supplies, such as paper for photocopiers or toner for printers, the team should look at where those supplies are housed.

The machines used in libraries often require staff assistance in order to monitor use, teach patrons how to use them, trouble-shoot problems, replace supplies, and so forth. The design must account for staff access within the immediate area and from other work areas. The facility's design should also make it easy for staff to remove and repair the equipment. Furnishings, such as mobile carts for quick replacement of broken equipment, could provide design alternatives.

Principal machines and machine areas include:

- Microforms
- Audio-visual equipment
- Audio-visual materials (especially those requiring security, like video cassettes)
- Public use microcomputers
- CD-ROM work stations
- Office machines
- Public photocopiers and change machines

OTHER PHYSICAL ASPECTS

Physical considerations and design issues in library buildings are very wide ranging. Some factors to examine include:

- Signage, both inside and outside the building, and the relationship between signage and lighting.
- Parking. Is it adequate and safe? Is access to the building from the parking lot simple and direct?
- Exterior lighting and user security
- Appearance, lighting, noise, and so forth
- Maintenance and custodial facilities. Some design features may be beautiful but difficult to clean and maintain
- Restrooms and lounges
- Access for the disabled and temporarily handicapped
- Adequacy of mechanical devices (heating, temperature control, humidity, interior lighting, and so forth)
- Seating. Is there enough of the right kind?
- Meeting rooms. Are the furnishings adequate? Is access and control appropriate?

CONDUCTING THE STUDY

If the evaluation team has done its homework and thoroughly planned the study, most of the hard work is done. The most important, and most difficult, aspect of a post-occupancy evaluation is developing and refining the research design. Creativity is exercised in devising and testing the instruments, selecting the sample, and resolving logistical problems.

Once those critical decisions have been made, the actual collecting of data becomes systematic. Administering questionnaires, observing behavior, and measuring environmental conditions become almost mechanical tasks. They require more patience and clerical skills than creativity and professional expertise. Nonetheless, there are a number of concerns that must be addressed even at this stage.

RIGOR AND RELEVANCE

Although data collecting may settle into a routine, the research team must stay alert to potential problems. All aspects of the study should be impartial, objective, systematic, and fair. The evaluators should insure that any potential bias or preconceptions are kept in check.

There are any number of fine textbooks and articles that provide guidance to achieving rigor and that spell out the details for sound, accurate methods. An excellent book on methods of gathering data for post-occupancy evaluation is *Methods in Environmental and Behavior Research*, (Robert B. Bechtel, Robert W. Marans, and William Michelson, 1987). The chapter "Evaluation of Designed Environments: Methods for Post-Occupancy Evaluation" by Craig M. Zimring, (page 270–300) is especially valuable.

While rigor should be pursued in all aspects of the study, blind reliance on scientific impartiality can sometimes get in the way of producing a useful post-occupancy evaluation. A design that does not allow for flexibility and common sense can result in a study that is no longer relevant to the library or the broadercommunity.

Random sampling, for example, typifies the kind of rigor that should be a part of nearly every study. Yet, a more cost effective and arguably more realistic measure of sentiment can be achieved by purposely selecting respondents or people to interview.

A random sample of library employees might not select any representatives from archives or the audio-visual department because of the small size of those units. These two departments might, however, play a central role in the library and the new facility. Relevance and common sense would suggest to the practical evaluator that someone from those two small departments should be contacted. Similarly, interviews with library users should include representatives of all significant minority or leadership groups, even though they might not turn up in a random sample.

Small groups can often point out shortcomings as well as large groups. The evaluation does not need a randomly selected sample of 10,000 users to tell it that the audio-visual collection is hard to find or that there are not enough lounge chairs. As Tom Peters pointed out in *Thriving on Chaos: Handbook for a Management Revolution* (1988), effective listening can be done on a very small scale.

A practical, action-oriented evaluation should always be relevant to practicing librarians in real libraries. As Daish wrote, "The methods in the literature tend to be research based—emphasizing the scientific method which requires care, objectivity, and usually time. In contrast the methods favoured in practice are quick, pragmatic and frequently subjective. To evaluate buildings as efficiently and comprehensively as possible with limited resources, methods need to be found which have the rigour of scientific method yet have some of the speed and pragmatism of current practice methods" (Daish et al., 1982, p. 79).

POLITICAL CONCERNS

Libraries are political organizations. This is never more obvious than in the funding, design, and construction of a new building. Politics can influence who the evaluators are able to collect information from and the candidness of their participation. As noted earlier, cooperation and support should be sought early in the evaluation and then developed and maintained throughout the process.

Evaluators can mediate between different groups from time to time, but they can also find themselves caught in local skirmishes. One evaluator noted that "extreme power differences, such as between a corporate board of directors and secretaries, may make such mediation impossible." He cited commentators who noted that reconciling differences of this depth was like trying to negotiate between slaves and slave owners on an eighteenth-century plantation (Zimring, 1987, page 286). The study is better served when the evaluators anticipate and take measures to avoid this kind of situation.

REPORTING AND DISSEMINATION

A post-occupancy evaluation is useless unless the evaluators present the findings in a way that can be used. A post-occupancy evaluation of libraries is not a theoretical exercise, and its recommendations for action must be practical. The language should be clean and free of jargon. Graphics and charts can help clarify detailed data. Microcomputer-based systems, including spreadsheet charts and desk top publishing, can help improve the presentation.

Zimring pointed out that reporting begins almost at the inception of the study. Key figures must be kept informed throughout the planning and evaluation process. It is not a good idea for the evaluation team to fade out of sight for two or three months as, for example, when writing the report. The sponsors or the staff could feel disappointed or even that they are the victims of a budding conspiracy (Zimring, 1987, page 281).

Different kinds of reports will help disseminate the findings. Small group meetings and discussions may be among the best ways to share findings with the community served by the library. The discussions that take place at these meetings could be incorporated into subsequent written reports.

Several reports, each varying in length, might be used. A multivolume report might have complete documentation of the questionnaire results, interview comments, and detailed environmental data. A shorter twenty- to fifty-page summary might be the main vehicle for communicating the findings. Still shorter documents, including posters, can be used for other groups.

Evaluators should not overlook the possibility of publishing their studies. Post-occupancy evaluations are frequently published in architectural journals, and evaluations of library buildings could add a great deal to the library literature. Journals oriented toward particular types of libraries or management concerns could be appropriate vehicles for shorter summaries of findings. Clearinghouse and depository agencies, such as ERIC, could be appropriate for longer reports.

Dissemination is often the weakest part of post-occupancy evaluations. Funding authorities, library organizations, and others can do a great deal to encourage or require both the evaluation of new buildings and the sharing of findings with the broader library community.

Dissemination of information or publication means that library planners, designers, and others can benefit from the post-occupancy evaluation. Future problems could be avoided and better libraries built. The methods of evaluation could also be improved by sharing information. Others planning post-occupancy evaluations could model the study, or portions of it, after earlier studies, thereby saving time, energy, and money.

Previously developed and tested questionnaires or other data collection instruments could be used in evaluations. Over time, use of the same or similar questionnaires could lead to comparisons between libraries and establishment of norms (Zimring, 1987, page 289).

ASSESSING THE PROCESS

The evaluation of library buildings requires one final feedback loop (Daish et al., 1983). This step asks the team to evaluate the evaluation, that is, to examine how well the process worked and to consider where it could be improved. Some questions that could be asked include:

- Did the evaluation achieve the goals established for it?
- What barriers to a good evaluation were encountered?

- How can those barriers be overcome?
- What were the strengths in the process?
- What were the weaknesses in the process?
- How could the evaluation process be made more effective?
- How could the evaluation process be made less costly?
- How could the evaluation process be done more quickly?
- How could the evaluation process be more objective?
- What will you do differently the next time?

15

A Post-Occupancy Evaluation of the Lucy Robbins Welles Library, Newington, Connecticut

The Lucy Robbins Welles Library, located in Newington, Connecticut, completed a major expansion and renovation in February 1988. The objectives of the facility, as stated in the 1984 building program, were:

- To be an information center where facilities meet the needs of individuals, businesses, community organizations, students, and local government.
- To be up-to-date in the latest developments in library technology including automated circulation, acquisitions, catalogs, and information systems.
- To be accessible to the handicapped.
- To be a community multi-purpose space where the library and local groups will have accommodations to hold programs, exhibits, and meetings.
- To have adequate work space for in-house library functions including administration, technical processing, and custodial services designed to make effective use of staff time.

The expansion added 14,000 square feet and renovated an existing 10,000 square foot building originally constructed in 1939. The book capacity more than doubled (from 50,000 to 102,000), the number of seats for library users expanded from 95 to 153, and meeting room capacity jumped from sixteen to 126 seats.

Newington is a residential community of 28,841 (U.S. Bureau of the Census, 1980) approximately fifteen miles south of Hartford, the state capital. It is a highly educated community with many adult residents engaged in managerial and professional work in surrounding towns. Less than two percent of the population are members of recognized minorities. Newington's public library was established in 1939.

The building consultant, Nolan Lushington, and Maxine Bleiweis, its director, worked closely on this project. The expansion and renovation was designed by Kaestle Boos Associates of New Britain, Connecticut. The post-occupancy evaluation was suggested and arranged by Lushington with the support of an LSCA grant administered the State Library of Connecticut. Planning for the evaluation began in the fall of 1988, with the first data gathered in January 1989. The study was completed in September 1989. The goals of the post-occupancy evaluation, as developed by the library staff, were:

- To test a variety of methods for post-occupancy evaluation
- To achieve positive feedback from the public
- To improve the library building
- To have a basis for long term planning

Since the primary goals emphasize outside appraisals, methods were used to gather information about the library and perceptions of the library from users, community leaders, and outside experts. Questionnaires were mailed to a sample of registered library users, while young library users and others were interviewed in the children's room. Two focus group meetings were held, and an architect and a library planning consultant, neither involved with the planning or design of the building expansion and renovation, were brought in to evaluate the building.

PERFORMANCE MEASURES

Performance or output measures were used to compare services provided to library users before and after completion of the addition and renovation. Use of the library jumped at least one-third and, in some cases, nearly doubled. The number of people entering the library rose 89 percent, moving from 450 to 850 users per day. One of the largest increases (63 percent) was in the number of reference questions. This probably reflects the redesign and improved location of the new information desk. The personnel budget and total library expenditures kept pace with the increase in use.

	1986–87	1988–89	Change
Output Measures		284,930	+38%
Circulation	205,858	22,792	+63%
Reference transactions	13,956	12,335	+14%
Registered borrowers	10,797	850	+89%
Daily traffic count	450	1,549	−25%
Interlibrary loan requests	2,062		
Budget/Staffing		$634,332	+70%
Total budget	$373,997	$406,490	+62%
Personnel budget	$251,483	11	+38%
Full-time staff	8	250	+77%
Part-time hours per week	141		
Base Statistics		24,000	+140%
Building square footage	10,000	102,000	+104%
Book capacity	50,000	153	+62%
Seating	95	29,600	+1%
Population (est.)	29,220		

Only the number of requests for interlibrary loans (ILL) declined. This 25 percent drop (from just over 2,000 per year to 1,549) was not expected given the increased traffic and awareness of the library following the reopening. Fewer ILL requests may reflect improved satisfaction with the facilities and improved perception of collection quality. It may also derive from improved access and ease of using the existing collection in the larger, more efficient building.

COMMUNITY SURVEYS

Two surveys were conducted: a questionnaire was mailed to a sample of adult users and interviews were conducted with users of the Children's Room.

Adult Questionnaire Survey

Methods.   A sample of 100 registered borrowers was randomly selected by a program on the library's computer circulation system. Two former employees were removed from the sample. A four-page questionnaire, cover letter, and stamped, self-addressed envelope was mailed to the 98 remaining on May 5, 1989. A follow-up letter and second questionnaire was sent May 17 if no response was received.

Questionnaires were returned by 73 respondents, although four were discarded because they were not completed or the respondent indicated the wish not to participate in the study. The final usable sample came to 69 of the 98 who were mailed questionnaires, or 70.4 percent.

A relatively small sample makes it possible to distribute a high-quality, personally addressed questionnaire and cover letter and to follow up nonresponses, if necessary. The sample size used in this study compares favorably with samples used in other post-occupancy evaluations. A major study of a Federal Office Building in Ann Arbor surveyed 113 residents (of 174 in the original sample) out of a population exceeding 100,000 (Marans and Spreckelmeyer, 1981, page 15).

Results.   The respondents appeared to represent the range of Newington residents and Welles Library users. Over fifty percent (35 of 68 respondents) were aged 25 to 44 years, 17.6 percent (12 respondents) were aged 45 to 65 years, 14.7 percent (10 respondents) were 66 or older, 11.7 percent (8 respondents) were 18 to 24 years, and three respondents were 17 or younger.

Most respondents were regular library users. Over half (36 of 68) said they usually used the library more than once a month, while 32 said they used the library less than once a month. Most visits were brief: 39 (55.7 percent) said their visits were less than 30 minutes; only eight (11.4 percent) usually spent more than an hour.

Users of the Lucy Robbins Welles Library were very pleased with the new building. On four-point Lickert-like scales, all respondents who had an opinion agreed or tended to agree with the following statements:

- The exterior design is attractive.
- The sign in front of the building helps in locating the library.
- The exterior lighting is adequate.
- The library is easy to find.
- It is easy to return and check out materials.
- The information desk is easy to find.

Ninety to 95 percent of the respondents agreed or tended to agree with the following:

- The entrance is easy to find.
- The interior of this library is attractive.

- The library has enough places to sit.
- The library is arranged so that it is easy to get to the items I want.
- The library is well lighted in the areas with tables and chairs.
- There are enough signs to help me find what I need.
- The library has a comfortable temperature.
- The young adult area is easy to find.

Although a vast majority was favorably impressed with all areas of the building, the most criticism was directed toward noise, parking, crowded areas, and restrooms. Five (7.4 percent) disagreed with "the library has sufficient quiet areas" while five (10.2 percent of those answering this question) agreed or tended to agree that "the library feels crowded." They noted crowding at study carrels in the evenings, at the check-out desk, the children's play area, and cassette displays near the study area.

Five respondents (10 percent) also disagreed or tended to disagree that "the restrooms are accessible." Several wrote that they were unhappy having to ask at the circulation desk for keys to the restrooms.

Parking was probably the greatest source of displeasure, although a minority criticized the parking situation. A third of the respondents (19 of 57) disagreed or tended to disagree with "there is adequate space in the library parking lot" and 11.1 percent could not agree that "the parking area is convenient." On the other hand, fully two-thirds of the respondents thought that there was adequate parking and nearly 90 percent found the parking convenient. Safety did not seem to be a problem: Over 90 percent agreed that "the parking lot is well lighted after dark," and 96.2 percent agreed that "the parking lot is safe." Four of 26 respondents (15.4 percent) disagreed or tended to disagree that "there is adequate parking for handicapped users." Users favorably mentioned availability of parking in nearby lots and cited problems with speeders taking a short-cut through the parking area.

Seating preferences varied. Most indicated no preference or said their choice would depend on the type of work they were doing at the time. Among those with a preference, 19 preferred carrels, 16 lounge chairs, and 5 chairs at a larger table.

Most users (49 of 68) had not attended a meeting in the community room or the smaller meeting room on the second floor. Among the 19 who had, strong majorities indicated that the rooms were attractive, not too hot or cold, were well lighted, had comfortable chairs, and were well located. Three respondents out of 15 answering agreed or tended to agree that "it was difficult to hear the program in the meeting room." One said that the ventilation system was noisy.

Traditional library use patterns predominated in the respondents' reasons for coming to the library. Most came to browse (52 respondents), to check out library materials (57), or look for specific material or information (59). Many came to consult the reference collection (38), use the photocopier (36), or ask for help from the reference librarian (35). Fewer patrons came to read magazines or newspapers (23), to bring a child (20), study using their own materials (13), use the library for work related activity (11), or use the young adult area (6 respondents).

Users were given a seven point Lickert-like scale (1 poor to 7 excellent) to answer the question, "Overall, how would you rate this library building?" All respondents but one scored the building a 5 ("good") or better. Twelve respondents gave the building a 5, 30 gave it a score of 6, and 26 respondents gave the building a 7, the highest score. One respondent gave the building a 3 or "fair" appraisal. The average was 6.16 on the seven-point scale.

Volunteered comments reflected the positive evaluations on the questionnaires. Several praised the attractive decor and said they used the library more since the expansion and renovation. One wrote, "The building is about the nicest we have seen—Newington should be proud of their nice addition to the town." Other comments included: "It has such a pleasant atmosphere that I plan to visit more often," and "It encourages more browsing and it allows a more comfortable setting. The library is a delight."

At least five respondents noted that the improved organization made the library easier to use:

"It is much better organized, easy to find items. It saves time."

"I visit the library more frequently and am more aware of what the library offers in the way of reference materials."

"I like the atmosphere. I never feel stuffy. Everything is very easy to find and I like the interior a lot. It's a very pretty place."

Two respondents said they preferred the old library and thought that the renovated library had lost some of its friendly, homey atmosphere. But many more cited the friendly service orientation of the staff. One wrote, "I was one of those people who was reluctant to change the library, probably because I tend to dislike change. It is obvious that the new library serves the town much better."

Children's Room Interviews

Methods.   This survey was conducted at different times on four different days during May 1989. The interviewer was instructed to purposively sample (i.e., nonrandomly select) as wide a range of users as possible.

The respondents included children aged eight years and older and adults who were either using the materials alone or accompanying a child. All interviews were conducted in the children's room.

Results. Forty-one users agreed to participate in the study: 8 were aged 8–10, 17 aged 11–18, and 16 respondents were over 18 years old. Most (36 of 41) reported that they used the library more than once a month. About half of the nonadult users (12 of 23) said they were accompanied by an adult; 11 children came to the library alone.

The overwhelming reason for coming to the Children's Room was to "pick out materials to borrow" (33 respondents). The library's ownership of two computers was given as the reason 14 came to the Children's Room. Seven came to do school homework, two came to use an encyclopedia or to browse drawing books, and five were in the room to "read," although the materials were not specified. Story hours attracted 9 users and 13 found the room's toys attractive. Many children attending story hour were the same ones who reported playing with the toys.

All users reported that the Children's Room was easy to find, although many said they originally asked a staff member for directions. Three-quarters (31 of 41) said materials were easy to find. Ten respondents indicated they occasionally had difficulty locating materials. Nearly all (37 of 40 responding to this question) thought that the materials were easy to reach; i.e., that the shelves were not too tall or short; 3 indicated mild difficulty reaching materials. The information desk was also a good height for all but two of the respondents.

Comfortable chairs and couches were the top choices for places to read (10 preferring chairs and 8 preferring couches). Seven read at tables and 2 at carrels. Those writing or taking notes preferred the carrels (11 responses) or the tables (9 responses), although two users of the children's room said that they like writing while sitting on one of the couches. All but 3 respondents thought the seating was adequate.

Nearly all (38 of 41) knew where the bathroom was located, although one user thought the doors were too heavy for children to open. The same number agreed that the signs were easy to read. Thirty-nine were content with the lighting and 2 more said the lighting was usually bright enough. About a third said they had used the listening or video equipment at one time or another.

Summary. Users of the children's room, both adults and youngsters, were largely pleased with the facility. Materials and facilities were judged easy to find and use. All furnishings and materials received considerable use and approval. Most users came to the library for traditional reasons: to borrow books and other items. A surprising number (14 of 41) came to use the computers. Another mild surprise is the popularity of the couches, which were used by adults and children, and even by some users writing papers. In contrast to the observation of the library planner (see below), a heavy majority of respondents thought that seating was adequate.

FOCUS GROUPS

Focus groups are often used in marketing and election campaign research. In contrast to questionnaire and interview surveys, this technique allows the researcher to probe and explore for deeply held convictions and attitudes. Because subjects are interviewed in a group, considerable interaction and cross-stimulation takes place. Most focus group meetings require two to three hours to conduct. The interviews and discussions for this study took place in January 1989. These summaries are taken from the longer focus group reports.

A SUMMARY OF THE FOCUS GROUPS' REPORTS
by Louise Blalock

Objective, Sample, and Methods

The focus group studies took a subjective and qualitative approach to discovering the impact of the new library building on its users. The focus group format was chosen for its ability to combine personal, in-depth opinions with a round table discussion and the sharing of various points of view. Respondents were asked to discuss their use of the library and the contribution the new building made to meeting their library service and information needs.

Thirteen library users shared thoughts about the old library, what they liked about the new library, and what they used in the new library, and they rated library features. They offered concerns and suggestions for future considerations and discussed using the new library. The participants represented a variety of ages and interests as well as intensity of library use. All were eager to be included in this phase in the Newington Library's post-occupancy evaluation, and they participated actively in the discussion. A focus group was also conducted for the library staff.

Summary and Conclusion

Library users, staff, and administration recognized the need to improve a limited and inadequate facility. The successful incorporation of the older facility into the expanded and renovated new building helped those who cherished the ambiance of the old library to feel at home in the new library. Everyone expressed satisfaction that a beautiful and functional library was built for the Newington community. Increased use by residents attests to this achievement. All users reported more frequent visits to the library, and more use of the library by the whole family. Staff members received positive feedback from their clients and perceived a significant increase in overall library activity. Use of neighboring libraries by Newington residents had been reduced by 60 percent, and attendance doubled since the new building opened.

There was some dissatisfaction. Library users and staff would have preferred a larger community room to allow for growth in programming activity. Some staff would have preferred a larger children's room, and most staff believed a main floor location for the children's room, rather than the new second-level location, would have enhanced library services to children. However, library users, staff, and administration cited pre-existing constraints in the building program and acknowledged the necessity of compromise.

In order of most frequently mentioned items, library users expressed the most satisfaction with the new reference area, space for a variety of activities in the new children's room, the new book area, the new area for teenagers, the new circulation desk, and the array of seating options throughout the library, including study carrels.

Two principal dissatisfactions emerged from the focus group discussion: the parking facility and locked restrooms. Feelings ran high on these two topics. All participants expressed safety concerns about the parking, which is separated from the library entrance by a road used for vehicular traffic. They believe crossing the public road to gain entrance to the library is hazardous, especially after dark. Those whose length of stay averages an hour or more in the library find the locked restrooms inconvenient, especially older people who are embarrassed to ask for the key repeatedly. All in the user focus group questioned the necessity of keeping the restrooms locked since they believe there is almost no incidence of vandalism in the library.

Library users, overall, were positive about the library facility, and had found many more satisfactions than dissatisfactions in discussing library features.

Staff expressed satisfaction with improved work space, more meeting and program space, the new reference area, the area for teenagers, and the study rooms. Staff perceive an up to seventy-five percent increase in reference use by the public. They attribute this increase to the new resources and equipment now available, and to the improved design of the reference area which has made the area more convenient for users and effective for staff.

Staff also commented on improved reference service in the children's room since the desk no longer serves a dual function as both circulation point and reference desk in the children's room. They endorsed the new centralized circulation desk on the main level which has freed children's services staff from the circulation function and allows them to focus on reference and reader's advisory work.

Some staff expressed dissatisfaction with the location and size of the children's room, which they experience as isolated from the rest of the library and smaller than the children's room in the old library. Most staff believe the location of the children's room on the second level is a compromise, and service to middle school aged children who need to use the resources of the teen and adult areas would have been better provided by a main floor location for the children's department.

All staff expressed some feelings of being out of contact with the children's department as well as with technical services, and believed the former central location of work space created an integration mechanism for staff. This loss is keenly felt, although the considerable improvement in overall working conditions is a high satisfier. Other integrating mechanisms such as task forces and shared tasks or functions or job sharing and job rotation may serve to decrease the sense of being separated.

Two features, lighting and temperature control, were areas of concern to staff. Cold drafts from the main door bothered staff at the circulation desk. The staff is confident, however, that this will be corrected. Reference staff and others found lighting in the reference area a problem. The combination of overhead and task lighting appears to cause discomforting vision adjustment among staff. Staff also believed the children's room was poorly lit and nconvenienced users. These problems were also cited by administration. They were not mentioned by the user group as dissatisfactions.

Low shelving for new books was mentioned by staff as a problem for seniors. Staff believed future use of top and bottom shelves (now empty) in the stacks also will disadvantage seniors.

Staff perceive increased use of the library by three user groups: business people, teens, and seniors.

Staff have received positive feedback about the expanded and renovated library. They are pleased that use of the hometown library has increased, and they are proud of their new ability to serve the community.

Although two important productivity gains, attendance and circulation, have been measured, staff were uncertain about their own productivity improvement. Performance ratios (quantity of service to cost) could also be used. A comparison of selected activities or outputs at unit cost for a post new building year with a pre new building year would document staff efficiences in the new library. Use of these efficiency measures as well as measures of user perception sampling and other selected qualitative user outcomes would give further evidence of the success of the Newington Library.

Library users, staff, and administration are enthusiastic about the new library and share a feeling of accomplishment. Use is up and morale is high. The Director expressed it well in remarking "how it all comes together"—beauty, function and community approval.

EXPERT EVALUATION

Two experts on library planning and design were selected to evaluate the Welles library building. The library planner, Joseph A. Ruef, is a public library administrator who has participated in the development of several library programs. Richard Schoenhardt, the architect, has been responsible for the design of several library buildings in Connecticut.

THE PLANNER'S REVIEW
by Joseph A. Ruef

Basically, the Newington Public Library is one of the most functional, attractive and interesting library buildings in the State.

Those who planned it and implemented it performed a praise-worthy job. I have visited the library repeatedly—twice in August [1989] for several hours, spoken to a number of staff members, and examined the building rather carefully; so this is not a quick judgment.

Particularly noteworthy are the following (the list is not meant to be complete):

- the use of marketing concepts,
- emphasis on A/V materials prominently displayed,
- the young adult area which invites use but not loitering,
- the circulation desk which hides wires and has steps for children,
- the imaginative transition from the popular area to the reference area,
- the location of InfoTrac and periodicals on cassettes,
- the quantity of seating which is spread out rather than concentrated in one spot
- the numerous study carrels,
- the work flow and amount of space in the workrooms and offices, the location of the three copiers,
- the use of the old building for reference and magazine reading,
- the entrance to the children's room with coat hangers and program announcements,
- the area for micros in the children's room,
- the reading bench in the children's room by the window,
- the location of meeting rooms for Board meetings, and especially children's programs.

This next list includes problems areas, some of which could hardly be avoided; others are in the process of correction. In some cases, I will also indicate how corrections could be made, if so desired.

New Books—I've seen people craning their heads or going down on all fours! The easiest solution seems to be two more benches.

Reference Desk—It behaves like a fortress! Reference librarians cannot easily volunteer help to patrons who look lost. Its main advantages are beauty, space and high visibility. I would recommend, however, drastic surgery; lower it, but more importantly, open it up! Other problems include the difficulty of reference librarians, who are outside of it, to reach the phone inside of it; patrons having no place to sit down while the reference librarian is answering phones or other patrons' questions.

Signage—It is attractive, but in my opinion, too small. Suggestion: Buy large banners which will better indicate where new books are, picture books, conference room, etc. Their locations may be obvious to staff and those who use the library frequently, but not to others. Also, large signs for the different types of A/V would be helpful, i.e. CDs, audiocassettes, videocassettes.

Elevator—It can be closely watched from the circulation desk. Staff claims there have been no problems with children getting stuck or riding up and down. However, in the limited time I was there, I saw a couple of scenes with children which made me feel a bit uncomfortable. I assume the elevator can be locked at certain times.

Future Expansion—How can the building be expanded in fifteen or twenty years, if necessary? Not too early to give this some thought.

Paperbacks—While I have no quick remedy, I did find the paperbacks on the regular stacks unsightly and difficult to use. More racks may be needed.

Storage—Not enough of it; again, I have no quick remedy.

Parking—Apparently, this is a problem being addressed. It is fairly urgent. When I was last at the library, there was a car accident at the intersection. People backing up have to fight the through-traffic. Also, when one leaves the library parking lot, it is easy to get lost! Road signs would be helpful.

Book Stacks—They appear efficient, but I can't help wondering whether non-fiction should not be closer to the reference area. The library director told me she gave the problem a lot of thought. Perhaps more discussion will be needed on this issue as time progresses.

Bathrooms—They appear graffiti-proof. The difficulty is the need to ask for keys. I have no big problem with the present solution, but perhaps the reason for the control should be explained to patrons on a sign on the outside of the doors. Another possibility would be to experiment for two or three weeks with unlocked bathrooms. There is no question that it is annoying to have to ask for a key if one has to go in more than once! Also, towel dispensers should be lowered for wheelchairs users; this should be easy.

Children's Room—I frankly had some difficulty with that area. First, I could not find any adult seating, although many adults use the children's area (mostly mothers). There were two adult armchairs, but children like them and were seated in them! Adults have trouble going through the picture books. They go down on their knees and crane their necks! The realia was out of the way. The children's librarian explained to me that realia are not considered important. I was not convinced; toys can, after all, be very educational and give an added dimension to children's services. Which leads to the issue of the sliding pond and the house. The sliding pond looked dangerous to me: one child kept jumping off the top instead of sliding down! I am also not sold on the house in the corner. Naturally, most children enjoy this; such equipment makes it look as though the library is "with it." Perhaps these items could be replaced by fun equipment which is safer and just as enticing. A small committee of people who work in the children's room could make recommendations. The children's room is crowded and much of it is occupied by unimaginative stacks which in some cases can't even be controlled visually from the desk. Could a number of stacks be removed temporarily to allow for a more spacious feeling?

Admittedly, it is easier to criticize than to build. My negative remarks make me feel somewhat guilty, especially since the building is largely such a triumph. I console myself with the thought that some of my criticism may lead to improvement in the next few months and years.

I close with the observation that the Board, Director, staff, architect, consultants, and all others who helped to produce this building have every reason to feel proud of themselves. Bravo for a good job!

THE ARCHITECT'S REVIEW
by Richard Schoenhardt, AIA

The most successful features of this building are:

Site

- Appropriately sized and located with an identification sign at the corner of the site which is readily seen by automobile traffic.
- Entrance area that is clearly identified by architectural form with steps and flanking curbed walls that direct attention to the entrance in an inviting and welcoming manner.
- One way traffic entrance to the site which provides safe and easy access.
- Discrete separation of service traffic to a visually shielded receiving and dumpster area.
- Preservation of mature specimen trees.

External Architecture

- Preservation of handsome traditionally styled existing library building and sensitive integration of new with old.
- Excellent match of new soft red colored brick with old building brick, while repeating Flemish bond pattern.
- Repeat of existing details in new building including brick corner quoins, wooden shutters, traditional shutter hardware, and roof edge details.
- Sheltered porch entrance, with weather protected bookdrop.
- Sign at entry with hours of operation and notices.
- Automatic doors for easy access for the handicapped and users with full load of books.

Internal Architecture

- Clear organization of functions at entry: view to circulation desk, entrance to meeting rooms, toilets, telephone and copier.
- Engaging view from entry into circulation desk, browsing, information desk and stack area.

- Soft, warm and pleasant color choices for carpet, walls, and furnishings.
- Exciting central skylighted area with bright sunlight and exposure of brownstone walls, slate roof, dormers and windows of the original building.
- Level changes between new and old building nicely arranged by ramp and stairs.
- Preservation of handsomely detailed original library rooms with their fireplaces, paneling and wood shelving.
- Clear organization of bookstacks in one integrated aisle system with well distributed lighting on all shelving levels and clear signing.
- Pleasant variety in selection and arrangement of furnishings.
- Nicely detailed, traditionally styled study carrels with built-in lighting.
- Young adult area centrally located to give important recognition to this age group, but in a secluded alcove with direct visual observation from the reference desk.
- Highly functional and efficient staff area that is located at the action core of the building adjacent to the circulation desk.
- Children's space that is interestingly subdivided and with an upper level entrance lobby that provides architectural entrance features to specialize this area. Materials are interestingly displayed for young users.
- Use of undivided glazing to separate staff offices at circulation desk and children's staff area provide for easy viewing and sense of openness.
- Use of many handsome refinished antique chairs and other furnishings.
- Dual height railing for stair to Children's area.
- Nicely scaled, traditional wall light fixtures with glass shades over built-in wood shelving in old reading rooms.

These features can be corrected as the circumstances allow:

Site

There is concern for safety of users crossing through traffic which passes between the entrance and the general parking lot. This could be relieved by closing the end of the entrance driveway between the building entrance and the service driveway and creating a pedestrian island to the parking lot. Through traffic would be directed to turn right into the parking lot prior to reaching the building entrance.

Interior Architecture

- Reduce excessive glare from the skylight by adding shading film to the glass and hanging vertical blind panels. This would prevent slanting sun rays from penetrating the space below. Also change white wall surfaces to a tan tone to reduce reflectance.
- Make signing to the Children's area access stair more attractive and exciting by the use of a banner. Also, decorate this stair's walls with banners or artwork. The access seems dull compared with the exciting area it leads to.

Lighting

- Correct for low light levels in work area behind the circulation desk by adding fixtures.
- Move strip of recessed fluorescent lighting over picture gallery wall further away from the wall to allow light to shine on pictures, and avoid excessive brightness on the wall above the pictures. "Wall-washing" fixtures are required.
- Correct for low light levels at card catalog and browsing area by adding fixtures.
- Correct for inadequate and poorly distributed lighting in sky-lighted atrium area by replacing wall fixtures with traditionally styled globe fixtures to be visually compatible with the post-top lights in this space.
- Correct for inadequate lighting over the Information Desk area by installing a suspended overhead system of tube lights similar to the shape used in the old reading rooms but with downlighting instead of uplighting.
- Correct for uneven lighting on stacks facing the study rooms by rearranging existing lighting and adding new units to form a continuous row.
- Correct for uneven lighting for signing at the ends of the bookstacks by adding and relocating fixtures.

- Correct for lack of light at the upper shelving in the Young Adults area by moving lighting closer to the shelving or adding fixtures.
- Change the utilitarian fluorescent wall fixture at the entrance corridor to the upper level meeting rooms to a type that has less glare and better appearance.

Mechanical

- The return air grille in the bookstack area on the lower level transmits a lot of noise from the nearby air handling unit. If the noise level reduction is desired, relocate the grille further from the unit and provide acoustically lined ductwork and bends.
- Air handling equipment rooms on the lower and upper levels are not totally insulated and might contribute to unnecessary heat losses in winter.

These features are not considered correctable:

- The view of the exterior end of the skylight looks industrial and would have been more consistent in design if it were a brick gable end.
- The handicapped access ramp is long (but this is unavoidable due to the site grade changes).
- The blast unit heater over the inner vestibule door is bulky and unsightly and might have been replaced by units built into side walls.
- The main meeting room seems undersized for this size library.
- The custom made study carrels were designed with desk heights to allow antique arm chairs to fit under. But this feature provides writing surfaces at 30.75 inches, which is 1.75 inches higher than normal. The Children's area carrels are the same height, but perhaps refabrication of these units would be feasible using armless chairs.
- Many tables are 30 inches high, one inch higher than usual.
- The building is not expandable due to site limitations. Acquisition of adjacent property is highly recommended.

Recommendations for future library projects:

- Consider the comments listed here.
- Consider providing lighting plans that generally provide for uniform lighting levels throughout area where the arrangement of furnishings is likely to change.
- If electrical and lighting plans are provided to suit a specific furnishings plan, carefully coordinate lighting with changes in the furnishings plan.

Conclusion

On balance, the Newington Library is an extremely successful project which provides a great abundance of well planned features. It is a pleasurable experience from the perspective of both architectural and library space planning concerns.

EVALUATING THE EVALUATION

The post-occupancy evaluation of the Welles Library achieved many of its goals. It also resulted in a number of unexpected benefits for the library, including a great deal of favorable publicity in the community and in the state. Several library users selected for the survey remarked that they were pleased that the library thought enough to ask their opinions. A high-quality, personalized cover letter and questionnaire may have helped. The evaluation study itself was the subject of an article in a statewide newspaper. Finally, the study contributed to our understanding of the evaluation process.

No one involved, whether administrators, staff, outside expert evaluators, or those collecting data, had ever participated in this kind of study. The evaluation was, to a large degree, a prototype. It was an opportunity to devise an evaluation process, to test it, and then share what was learned with a wider library community.

The evaluation itself was overwhelmingly favorable—almost flattering—to those involved in the design and construction of the Welles library. The study confirmed the need to make a number of minor adjustments or modifications to the facility. There were, however, no major surprises and only a few unexpected findings.

The methodology, however, was less predictable and yielded a few surprises. The collection and analysis of data could have been improved by following these recommendations:

1. *Select a Director.* Administrators or those responsible for the evaluation must hire or appoint someone to coordinate the study

who can be onsite for most, if not all, of the data collection. The evaluators and staff should have ready access to someone with the knowledge and authority to guide the study. The research cannot be done by automatic pilot or managed by remote control.

Those involved in the evaluation need guidance and counseling. They need to be trained in the objectives, purpose, and tools of the study. This can be especially true for the outside expert evaluators, who may be completely new to the process. Lack of training and supervision can mean that the evaluators drift in and out without bringing a common focus or understanding of the objectives to the study.

Communications and coordination of logistics can become a problem. A lack of a central resource person in the Welles Library evaluation, for example, meant that a revised and updated interview schedule never found its way to the interviewer, who was consequently forced to make important decisions about the interpretation of a flawed instrument.

2. *Planning is Critical.* Evaluators must allow adequate time to plan and coordinate activities. A bias for action, although highly desirable, can result in lost opportunity. The most common bias for action in library-related research is the perceived need to get some data—and that usually means mailing a questionnaire. In this evaluation, the questionnaire was devised and data collection begun before the focus group report was available. That report might have suggested important questions that could have been included in the survey.

3. *Maintain Objectivity.* There is a natural and understandable tendency for those involved in an evaluation to want to put the library in the best possible light. The staff of the library being evaluated may feel that they are disloyal if they point out shortcomings; outside evaluators may feel uneasy criticizing peers. Yet, if the process is to be valuable and not a white-wash, the team coordinator or director must insist on objectivity from all involved. This will require education about the goals and purpose of the study and training must include everyone involved.

4. *Resist the Temptation to Survey Everything.* It has been suggested that putting a questionnaire in the hands of a librarian is like placing a hammer in the hands of a youngster: everything looks as though it needs to be surveyed or hammered!

Not only is there a natural inclination to survey, the enthusiasm for questionnaires may also be responsible for the addition of many unnecessary questions to those instruments. For a successful study, all the questions should be directly relevant and useful to the evaluation. The instrument surveying users of the Welles Library children's room, for example, asked users, "Where are the books that you use?" Yet, questions like this have little bearing on the evaluation and add little to understanding the relationship between users and the facility.

Too often evaluators find that they have asked questions that serve no useful purpose or that are so ambiguous in their logic that the responses cannot be competently analyzed. Much time is also lost recording and totaling the responses to these less than valuable questions. The evaluation coordinator must ruthlessly fight to pare any proposed surveys.

Most library personnel are comfortable with questionnaire formats but less so with observational procedures. This familiarity may be the reason other, potentially better, procedures are not used more in library research. The evaluators must continually ask themselves whether a survey is the best way to collect data. The Welles Library evaluation, for example, asked users of the children's room questions about the height of shelving and the circulation desk. The respondents overwhelmingly reported that they had no trouble with the heights of the furnishings. The same information might have been collected more easily, quickly, accurately, and with less expensive by observing children using those furnishings.

Summary.   Most of these observations are interrelated. They emphasize the importance of good planning, training, and thoughtful exploration of the range of alternatives in order to find methodologies and techniques best suited for the goals of a specific evaluation. In many library organizations, especially those with personnel without experience in post-occupancy evaluation, the best way to achieve this is by selecting an on-site evaluation director who has the skills and authority to carry out the study.

A great deal was learned about the evaluation process in conducting this study. It was successful in testing a methodology, including the adaptation of procedures and instruments used in other studies. The experience will also be useful in developing strategies and tactics that can be used by others. Finally, the process confirmed that the best post-occupancy evaluations are those which embrace common sense and commonly established principles for systematic and objective data gathering.

Appendix

Yonkers Public Library Building Program Summary Report

A summary of a preconstruction analysis and planning document for the construction of a new building for the Yonkers Public Library, Yonkers, New York, prepared August 15, 1989.

INTRODUCTION AND OVERVIEW

The Purpose of This Study

In the spring of 1989 the Trustees of the Yonkers Public Library commissioned Nolan Lushington to evaluate facility requirements and develop a plan for construction of a new library building. This report is the product of an assessment of the goals and missions of the library system and the physical facilities needed to accomplish these objectives. Data for this report was collected through interviews with employees and officials, and analysis of local documents and regional statistical information.

The Community of Yonkers

The citizens of Yonkers actively participate in the affairs of their community. High educational achievement, above-average family incomes, and the occupational status of many residents contribute to a long tradition of support and use of the Yonkers Public Library system. Over a quarter of the residents (56,873) are registered users of the library.

Yonkers citizens see the public library as a valuable asset for educational advancement, independent study, and information for daily living, as well as a cultural and recreational resource for the entire community.

Yonkers is a mature suburban community of 193,800 (U.S. Bureau of the Census, 1987 estimate). While there are many tradition-rich older areas, community leaders are planning important new redevelopment projects for the city. The residents embody significant cultural and demographic diversity. The community is approximately 84 percent white, 10.5 percent black, 8.6 percent Hispanic, and 4 percent Asian.

Mission of the Yonkers Public Library

The projected library building and changes in physical facilities are derived from the mission and goals the public library has adopted in order to serve the community. The public library in Yonkers sees its mission to serve as a

- Popular library by providing materials for recreational and information needs of its citizens.
- Reference library for students, scholars, and members of the business community and other organizations

Secondary missions include:

- Independent Learning Center for citizens to continue a lifetime of learning.
- Community Activities Center.

Critical Analysis of the Getty Square Building

Community leaders have recognized the growing need for a new downtown library for over twenty-five years. The Getty Square Branch is located in Yonkers's central business district in a building formerly occupied by a department store. Although the staff has worked very hard since 1978 to adapt this building to provide good library services to the citizens of Yonkers, the aging four-story facility lacks the space and the design qualities necessary for modern library service.

Society and libraries have seen major advances in recent years, and the present lack of space creates major problems. Computers and other new information technologies, the proliferation of information, and the surge of opportunities for independent learning have all had a major impact on the need for additional space for services in the library.

Most critical of all, the current building does not offer off-street parking or any dedicated parking for library users. The lack of adequate parking space is a significant deterrent to use by residents who live outside the immediate area.

Major factors adversely affecting library service include:

- Lack of parking
- Site not easily accessible to many residents
- Building not designed for modern library service
- Aging facility; upkeep expensive
- Inadequate reader and study space
- Inadequate space for collections
- Insufficient space and electrical capacity for new technologies (computers, typewriters, CD-ROMs, etc.)
- Inadequate storage space
- Lack of adequate meeting space for public and staff
- Limited future growth space
- Overflowing nonfiction stacks
- Remote reference area on second floor
- Structural support for high-density storage insufficient

Summary of the Plan

The new building will be centrally located near City Hall and other governmental offices and agencies. The site is at the intersection of two major north-south and east-west arterials that feed into nearby parkways and expressways. It is also at the hub of public transportation with twelve bus lines within a two block area of the proposed library. High-rise and private residential housing is within easy walking distance. A major hospital, shopping, and other downtown attractions are also nearby. Plans for development projects on adjacent sites and elsewhere in the community could also channel traffic to the location.

The site allows access to pedestrians on at least two sides. The grade on the site may suggest the opportunity for a multilevel design that presents a simple, accessible, street-level entrance at the higher end of the site. At the same time, the location on Nepperhan Street, a major connecting thoroughfare, presents another opportunity. The library should be clearly visible to automobile traffic on Nepperhan. The new library can, by its physical presence on the hill, make an important statement to everyone driving up Nepperhan.

The site has several other advantages. With good management, the long-standing problem of inadequate parking can be solved. Widely used formulas based on area of the building and seating capacity indicate that at least two-hundred parking spaces (peak) must be allotted for library users. The site also allows for future expansion. Although the present building program provides for twenty years of future growth for the new library, the site permits flexibility and the possibility of an addition in twenty or thirty years.

The Yonkers design plan will emphasize the library's role as a popular library for the recreational and informational needs of the community in new and innovative ways. There will be a fast-service browsing area at the entrance for best-selling books, video cassettes, and other very popular materials. This lively, active area will be where library users can drop in, pick up a book, and be on their way in a few minutes. The library will also feature a coffee shop and book store, where residents can purchase books, magazines, and other popular items.

The library's role as a reference center for students, scholars, and members of the business community and the other traditional library roles will also be strengthened. Nearly all of these services for the adult citizens of Yonkers will be on the main or entry level of the library. These areas will be immediately visible from the entrance and the popular library yet they will be architecturally separate from the lively, quick-service popular library. This separation could be achieved by having the two areas on slightly different levels or by using glass or other design features to delineate that different library functions take place in these separate areas.

The entry level will hold reference services, including periodical indexes and job information collection. The government documents collection, magazines, and newspapers, and the adult fiction and nonfiction collections will also be on this level. There is one large bookstack area to hold most of the adult fiction and nonfiction collections. Separate areas for mysteries, westerns, science fiction, large-print materials, paperbacks, young adult materials, and Spanish-language materials will be nearby. In all, the entry level will have room for 100,000 books shelved on stacks 60" high with 48" aisles. It will have a variety of seating for 118 readers, with study carrels for another forty on a mezzanine overlooking the main floor.

Other levels in the new library will feature the children's area, with its pleasant garden view, an auditorium seating 250, and two smaller meeting rooms for groups as large as seventy-five and twenty-five. Offices and other administrative areas will also be located on another level, as will most storage and maintenance areas. Technical services and book processing will be done at another facility.

The major advantages of the new building include:

- With proper management, it provides adequate parking for residents.
- Site is easily accessible to residents from different parts of the city.
- Site is accessible to both pedestrian and automobile traffic.
- Design calls for integration of key library functions on the entry level.
- Building will be designed for modern library service.
- Cost of upkeep reduced.
- It provides a local history room to collect and preserve information on the diverse ethnic heritage of Yonkers.
- Adequate reader and study space.
- Adequate space for collections.
- Space for new technologies: computers, typewriters, CD-ROMs, etc.
- Adequate storage space.
- Adequate meeting space for public and staff.
- Room for future expansion if necessary.

Analysis of current service requirements and present facilities indicate that efficient service can be achieved by allocating functional areas in the library as noted in the following table:

Table 1.
Downtown Library Service Requirements

	1988 (Existing)	*2008* A.D.
Area	52,000 sq. ft.	77,000 sq. ft.
Seats (total)	125	192
adult		158
children		34
Program seats	90	250
Volumes (adult)	70,000	109,500
(children)	33,000	63,000

Table 2.
Area Requirements

Main Entry Level	45,800 sq. ft.
Circulation	2,000 sq. ft.
Popular library (3000 books)	3,000 sq. ft.

Table 2.
Area Requirements *(continued)*

Reading (118 seats on entry level, 40 carrels on mezzanine)	3,500 sq. ft.
Study rooms (6 individual, 3 group rooms)	500 sq. ft.
Reference (6,000 books, 50,000 compact storage)	15,300 sq. ft.
Branch administrator's suite	500 sq. ft.
Bookstacks (109,500 books)	11,000 sq. ft.
Entry-level non-assignable space (lobby, service vestibule, restrooms, storage, corridors, etc.)	10,000 sq. ft.
Other Levels	33,900 sq. ft.
Mezzanine (40 carrels)	1,200 sq. ft.
Children's services, total area	10,250 sq. ft.
Office	450 sq. ft.
Preschool (3,000 picture books)	1,500 sq. ft.
Browsing/reading (12 tables with seats)	1,500 sq. ft.
Reference (800 books, 16 seats at tables, 6 carrels)	1,000 sq. ft.
Bookstacks (63,000 books)	5,000 sq. ft.
Activity area (48 stackable chairs)	500 sq. ft.
Storage closet	400 sq. ft.
Local history room	1,000 sq. ft.
Program area (250 seats)	4,000 sq. ft.
Meeting room (75 seats)	1,000 sq. ft.
Meeting room (25 seats)	300 sq. ft.
Auditorium service area	300 sq. ft.
Administrative area	4,650 sq. ft. Total
Director	400 sq. ft.
Assistant director (2 offices, 200 sq. ft. each)	400 sq. ft.
Community services coordinator (and assistant)	300 sq. ft.
Building superintendent (and assistant)	300 sq. ft.
Business manager	200 sq. ft.
Secretaries (3 offices with 150 sq. ft. each)	450 sq. ft.
Business (work stations for 8 support staff)	700 sq. ft.
Graphics and print shop	600 sq. ft.
Administrative-board conference room	300 sq. ft.
Staff lounge	1,000 sq. ft.
Other levels nonassignable	10,000 sq. ft.
Public restaurant/book store	1,000 sq. ft.
GRAND TOTAL:	79,700 sq. ft.

THE ENTRY LEVEL

Functions and Activities

The entry level is the heart of the Yonkers Public Library. All users of the library will enter and leave the library through this level. It is the vibrant, bustling crossroads where every day hundreds of people come with their children on their way to a story hour or to pick up a popular video cassette or to ask a reference librarian a good way to stop a troublesome bathroom leak.

Excellent traffic flow and logical placement of service facilities are critically important. Design considerations should center on intensity of use factors. A design with open sightlines and the flexibility to modify facilities as service needs change contributes to a successful and efficient library. A self-service, user-friendly environment requires early attention to graphics, signage, and color guidance systems.

Most services and materials for adults are on the main or entry level of the library. Anyone entering the building will see the popular library at the entrance. The library user should also be able to easily identify the major service areas on the floor and the way to services and facilities on other floors. The circulation desk will be near the entrance lobby area, and within easy view of the front door is the public access catalog area. Circulation, reference, and most of the library's books will follow the popular library. This arrangement places those services most often used nearest the entrance and near to each other in what is called a hierarchy of use.

The entry level will also include offices for the circulation staff and reference staff, and a three-room suite for the branch administrator. Each of these offices should be located so that staff can easily and quickly

Entry Level Service Relationships

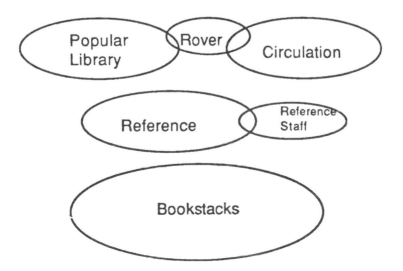

get to public service areas as the need arises. A staff rover will also assist the public in this area.

Lobby/Vestibule

This area must offer a positive welcome to the library. It should be efficient and businesslike in its design while also establishing the purpose and function of the library. Trees, growing things, and art work will help establish this ambiance. It will have locked and lighted glass display cases and announcement boards visible on entry listing hours, services, scheduled events, and other policy information. The lobby will have a book drop where library users can leave books after the library is closed. The book drop will have a built-in smoke detector and CO_2 extinguisher, and will be lockable so that it cannot be used during normal operating hours.

An area just off the lobby/vestibule and reasonably close to the circulation desk will have a number of public conveniences that, while important to some library users, are not central to the mission of the Yonkers Public Library. Public telephones, coin-operated photocopiers, change machines, a bulletin board and racks for displaying public service hand-outs, such as tax forms and community information, will be available here.

Popular Library

Someone entering the building will first see the popular library with its 3,000 best-sellers, compact discs, audio cassettes and videos. This is a quick service area designed to assist borrowers to find an item, check it out, and be on their way. There are no chairs, no magazines, and no newspapers in this 3,000 square-foot area.

The popular library is bright and upbeat. Although traffic flow and efficiency are important design considerations, the popular library should be attractive and pleasant. Greenery and art work are also appropriate here. This part of the library should resemble a modern book store, where books are displayed face out or on zig-zag shelving. Books are spread out with front covers displayed. Shelving will be 12" to 48" high and lighting will dramatically highlight materials. It is not an area for lengthy rumination or contemplation. The 5,000 video cassettes will require a bypass security/circulation configuration. This arrangement should not be obtrusive and should feed users to the circulation desk.

Circulation Area

The area inside the vestibule/lobby is devoted to circulation. The circulation area is an efficient, carefully designed work area where library users can return borrowed materials, check out newly found books, or inquire about the status of a reserve book. Work flow and efficient movement of library users are critical to the success of the library design. People checking out books and leaving the library should not interfere with those just arriving. The design of the desk and related areas and signage should establish the different functional areas for users.

The circulation area should be flexible enough to serve the wide variety of library users and their varying needs. For example, different counter heights are necessary for adults and children. There will be a separate section of the desk for checking out video cassettes. An area where prospective users can sit down to fill out a registration card is also a helpful design feature. There will be a typewriter station on the staff side for typing registration cards. The major portion of the desk will be of two heights: the public side will be 39 inches while the staff side will present a working desk height of 30 inches.

There will be no more than five staff members working at this area at one time. The circulation desk will have five terminal/workstations; four of the work stations will be at counter height and one will be desk height. Staff work stations at the circulation desk will be wired into automated online computer systems to accommodate CRT's, keyboards, light pens, laser bar-code readers, and printers mounted below counter level.

Circulation Staff Offices

Near the circulation area is the room where the staff processes materials, sorts mail, records the arrival of magazines and newspapers, files reports, maintains records, and otherwise manages the circulation function of the library.

The circulation staff supervisor will have a separate 75-square-foot office with desk/work station, two chairs, one four-drawer file cabinet and nine linear feet of single faced shelving. Three other supervisors will have desk/workstations (50 square feet each) in the staff office. Each employee working in this area will have a personal "homebase" work station which can be personalized. These nine workstations will be along 27 feet of counters. Each station will be a 30" high with 30" depth and will have shelving below and cabinets above. There will also be another 27-foot-long counter for the different functions performed in the area.

Rover's Station

This station is home base for a professional who directs users to the proper part of the library, answers questions, intercepts problems, and otherwise welcomes arrivals to the library. The rover librarian will most often move between the popular library, circulation desk, and the catalog area as needs demand. The rover station is a stand-up, counter-height station on the forward portion of the circulation desk, which is nearest the entrance and the popular library. It will have a counter-height stool, terminal/work station, telephone, and lockable drawer.

Public Access Catalog Area

The public access catalog area is between the circulation and reference areas and is visible from the entrance. The new Yonkers Public Library will not have a traditional card catalog, but will instead have a bank of computer work stations installed on counters so that most users can consult them while standing. At least ten public access catalogs will be in this area with another eight at the reference desk and others scattered throughout the different parts of the building. A number of stations at a lower height should be provided for disabled users.

Reference Area

Near the catalog is the reference area with its easily identifiable information desk. The reference department is where the people of Yonkers go for answers. It offers many different services, including information, business reference, and the job information center. Microform materials, indexes to periodicals, and magazines and newspapers are also located adjacent to the reference department.

The first thing a library user sees on entering this area is the information desk. This busy and occasionally noisy information service station is the place to get an answer to a specific question or assistance in using library materials. Telephone reference is an important part of the service offered here.

The 30-inch-high desk should face the arriving public with the bulk of the reference collection behind. The ready reference collection of frequently used materials and a microfiche cabinet will be kept on one side of a double-faced, 39-inch-high counter at the rear of the Information Desk. The public side of this counter will have eight public access computer stations and a microfiche reader.

The basic reference collection of approximately 6,000 volumes will be shelved on 100 double-faced sections arranged in 12-foot long ranges. The shelves will be at 42″ counter height so that users and librarians can pull a volume off a shelf and then consult the reference book on top of the shelving. It should be possible to add conventional 84″ shelving for expansion some time in the future.

The area will also include four atlas cases (flat-shelves with rollers), two dictionary stands, and a 6-foot wide wall-mounted relief map with pull-down map mounting racks above.

The vertical file of pamphlets and clippings will be stored in 24 4-drawer cabinets in this area. The job information center will have a 6′ free-standing bulletin board, two doubled-faced sections of 42-inch shelving, and two four-drawer vertical file cabinets. Compact shelving of back issues of periodicals and government publications will accommodate 50,000 items in 1,200 square feet. This 12-inch-deep shelving will only be accessible to staff. Reference seating will consist of twenty individual study carrels, twenty chairs at five 6-by-4-foot tables, and eight seats at the CD-ROM work stations in the index area.

Offices and a work area for the reference staff should also be in the same general area. This is where the staff orders reference materials, creates bibliographies, prepares presentations and otherwise plans and carries out its work. There will be a 75-square-foot office for the head of reference, eight work stations at 30-inch high counters, and room for possibly adding two more work stations in the general reference office. The reference staff will have the use of a 50-square-foot storage-supply closet, a key cabinet, and a coat closet with space for fifteen coats. Staff will also have the use of fifteen half or box lockers for personal possessions.

Indexes

Periodical and other indexes are important tools for research in libraries. They are the key to the contents of magazines, newspapers, and other media. The index area at the new Yonkers Public Library facility will hold two-thousand volumes on twenty stand-up tables or counters. Each will have a double shelf above the counter for the indexes. They should be placed against a wall. The index area will also include eight work stations for searching databases on CD-ROM systems. Each will include a personal computer work station, keyboard and CRT, printer, paper supply, and related documentation. Each work station will have a secretarial chair with casters.

Periodicals and Microforms

The library will subscribe to approximately 650 magazines. The current issues will be displayed face out on slant shelving. Twelve different newspapers will also be displayed. The new Yonkers facility will have eight microform reader-printers and forty microform cabinets, each measuring approximately 18 by 30 inches.

Audio-Visual Materials

Also near the information desk is a collection of audio records in three different formats. There will be display and storage for three-thousand compact discs (CDs) in two-level bins, another three-thousand audio cassettes in bins, and two-thousand phonograph records, also in two-level bins. Library users and the staff will use a public access catalog terminal in the area. There will not be separate listening facilities for use of these materials. Audio-visual formats are rapidly changing and evolving in libraries. There should be considerable flexibility in the audio-visual area to allow for the introduction and expansion of new formats over the coming years.

Branch Administrator's Office

The branch administrator's office will be warmly pleasant but professional and efficient. It will have plants and art and task and natural lighting with operable windows. Furnishings and equipment include a desk, chair with arms and casters, and 35 linear feet of wall shelving behind the desk. The office will also have four lounge chairs with two low tables for visitors, two four-drawer files, a credenza, and a 2-by-2-foot safe.

The secretary's ante room will have an L-shaped desk, swivel chair with arms and casters, a computer work station with printer. This room will have three lounge chairs and two low tables for waiting visitors, a photocopier, three four-drawer file cabinets, a 66 inch credenza, clock and planter. This room will also have a supply closet with shelving, a coat closet and two half or box lockers.

Bookstack Area

The entry level also houses the library's adult and young adult collections and the places where library users can read or examine the materials they retrieved from the reference collection or other parts of the library. In addition, it harbors a number of smaller, specialized collections and many quiet study areas (see section on seating below). The quiet areas and young adult area should be some distance from the main traffic flow, the elevators and the information desk.

There will be shelving for 109,500 volumes. The stacks will be 60 inches high and have 48-inch aisles (6 feet on center). In total, the 384 sections of double-faced shelving will require 11,000 square feet of area. The bookstack area should be constructed on grade or able to support 300 pounds per square foot live weight so that sometime in the future high-density storage can be installed. Compact shelving will make it possible to store over 300,000 volumes in this area in the future.

Stack aisles must be visible from staff areas for supervision by library staff. There should be a single, continuous, one-pattern bookstack area with graphic signs and integrated lighting for convenient access. These books are consecutively numbered and any break in the shelving pattern will be confusing to library users. A range of shelving should be a maximum of six three-foot-long sections to make it possible for readers to move easily from one aisle to the next.

Seating

The entry level will have a variety of seats in various locations. There will be 118 seats on the entry level floor itself and forty more at study carrels on an overlooking mezzanine. Seating includes sixty carrels, fourteen 6-foot-by-4-foot tables seating four readers each, and sixteen lounge chairs. In addition, there will be seating for eighteen more library users in the private and group study rooms on the entry level.

Reference:	
Carrels	20 seats
5 tables (4 chairs at each 6-foot-by-4-foot table)	20 seats
CD-ROM work stations	8 seats
Main reading:	
9 tables (4 chairs at each 6-foot-by-4-foot table)	36 seats
Lounge	16 seats
Study rooms	
Independent study rooms	6 seats
3 group study rooms (each with table and 4 chairs)	12 seats
Mezzanine:	
Carrels	40 seats
	Total: 158 seats

Mezzanine

The mezzanine will be a quiet study area overlooking the entry level. Forty study carrels grouped in gangs of four will be arranged so that the carrels are visible from staff locations below. There will not be elevator service to this area.

OTHER LEVELS: CHILDREN'S AREA

Children's services are very important at the Yonkers Public Library. This area will provide space for a full range of services for children from preschool age to twelve and their parents. The design and appearance of the Children's Room will make a lasting impression upon a child. There will be plants and a pleasant garden view. The area should express warmth and friendliness and suggest to parent and child that this is the place to come in order to satisfy information and recreational needs. Services and materials in this area must meet the needs of a wide variety of library users, from curious preschool toddlers through the rapidly changing preteenager. It must also serve the needs of parents who accompany their children to a story hour or other program or who come to this area with their children in order to find a book.

Functions and Requirements

There will be child-height fixtures in the restrooms, to be located immediately outside the children's area for close staff supervision. Both restrooms will have facilities for changing diapers and will be accessible to the disabled. There will also be child-sized coat racks for fifty children near the door. Two photocopiers will also be located near the entrance in order to minimize noise and distraction.

There should be access to the street separate from the adult areas so that the sometimes boisterous children do not disturb other library users. Traffic from this area will be channeled past the main circulation area so that children can borrow and return materials at the same desk as adults. Displays and seasonal decorations are an important aspect of the children's area. There will be tackable display walls along with locked glass display units in different parts of the room.

Service Areas

Because of the wide range of ages and activities here, there will be a number of special service areas within the larger area. These include:

Browsing/Reading. This part of the children's area will be near the bookstacks and will feature display racks for one thousand new books, a collection of Spanish-language materials, one thousand phonograph records and compact discs and two stations for listening to those recordings. Display shelving for thirty magazines and one thousand paperbacks will also be in this part of the children's area. It will have two computers for use by children and five computer work stations for the online public access catalog, which replaces the card catalog. There will be a variety of seating and table heights; in all there will be twelve tables seating forty-eight users in this area.

Reference. There will be two work stations for librarians assisting young library users to find what they need in the eight hundred reference books in this collection. The reference materials will be shelved on nine sections of counter-height shelving similar to the stacks used in the adult reference collection. Vertical file materials will be stored in three four-drawer cabinets. There will be four tables seating a total of sixteen children, six study carrels and two group study rooms seating six in each.

Activity Room. This is where crafts are made, story hours conducted, and videos shown. There will be a raised stage area and forty-five stackable chairs. Crafts will require four folding tables and a counter with a sink. An audio-visual closet will provide storage for a VCR, two projectors, and other equipment. The floor will be tiled and have floor drains so that it is easy to clean.

Preschool Area. This is a noisy, whimsical area near the entrance for children two to five years old. It's a fun place with child-sized furniture and a puppet stage, and a design that reflects the magic of childhood. There will be a small scale platform with carpeted stairs for children to climb and scramble on. There will be small "stimulus shelters" that toddlers can crawl into to find quiet and security. These cubby-hole areas serve a protective function by providing shelter from overstimulation. There will be a rocking chair in one section where a parent can read to a child.

There are three small collections of books in the preschool area. Divider shelving 42 inches high will hold three thousand picture books while a separate toddler section will have shelving for five hundred books and display racks for three hundred cassette books in plastic bags. A parent's corner will have a small collection of parenting books, magazines, and pamphlets parents can browse through while their children find a good book.

Other Features

There will be shelving for 63,000 books near the reading area on shelves 48 inches high (four shelves) with 48-inch aisles. The children's collection requires active weeding of worn-out and outdated materials. The net growth rate of approximately 1,500 volumes per year means that there will be 30,000 more volumes added to the current stock of 33,000 in twenty years. A 400-square-foot room with 15-inch industrial shelving will provide storage for exhibits and seasonal decorations and materials.

The children's area office must provide good supervision of all children's activities. The staff should, however, be able to adjust privacy in the office by closing blinds on a window and the door. The office will be 350 square feet in size with a separate 150-square-foot office for the administrator. The general office will have three work stations, two of which can be used with computer systems or typewriters, and room to add two more work stations in the future. There will be a counter where three people can work at one time. Working materials will be kept in three storage cabinets, two four-drawer file cabinets and six adjustable book shelves. The room will have six half-lockers, ten 6-inch-by-14-inch wall-mounted mail boxes, and a small coat closet.

OTHER LEVELS: LOCAL HISTORY COLLECTION

This collection and display area will contain books and documents important to the people of Yonkers. It will preserve the rich cultural and ethnic heritage of the community and record significant events in Yonkers' long and colorful history. Books written by local authors and selected memorabilia will also be collected and displayed here.

The room will contain a public access terminal and 60 linear feet of double-faced, 60-inch high shelving. Exhibits will be shown in two locked and lighted wall-mounted glass display cases and one 4-foot-by-4-foot free standing glass display case. There will be two work stations, three four-drawer file cabinets, and a 60-inch credenza. A custom atlas stand measures 42 inches in height by 27 inches in width and 40 inches in depth. Public seating will be four chairs at one 4-foot-by-6-foot table and three lounge chairs. There will be a locked storage closet with 50 linear feet of shelving. The staff will be able to control access or make the area available to the public by opening a double door or sliding open wide, tracked doors.

OTHER LEVELS: AUDITORIUM AND MEETING ROOMS

There are three sizes of rooms where residents of Yonkers can meet for a program or to discuss different issues. There is an auditorium or program area with 250 seats and two smaller meeting rooms seating 75 and 25 respectively. Passageways from the dock to this area should be wide enough to accommodate a piano (72 inches wide).

People attending programs or meetings in the auditorium and the two smaller meeting rooms should be able to enter and leave these rooms directly from the outside without going through the building. A separate entry means that programs can be held before the library opens or after it closes. It also means that readers and other library users will not be disturbed by large numbers of people entering or leaving the area.

Service Area

There will be restrooms, a coat area, and other service areas off a common corridor joining the auditorium and meeting rooms. There will also be a small kitchen area with sink and stove and a 60-square-foot storage room for audio-visual equipment and supplies. Near the public restrooms will be two small dressing rooms for performers.

Program Area

This is the place the community gathers to hear a lecture or to see a pageant put on by a local group. Films and musical productions may also be held in this area, and civic or other community groups might choose to hold their annual meetings or conduct hearings here. The auditorium will have a sloping floor and fixed, upholstered seating with wide-row aisles. There will be four flat areas for wheelchairs located in different areas of the auditorium. A stage with appropriate lighting and a projection room for showing films, slides and other media will be part of the design of the program area. Good acoustics and good sight lines are important. Although the program area has seating for 250, the design should also strive to make the room comfortable and inviting even when not filled to capacity.

Two smaller rooms seating seventy-five and twenty-five people should also be directly accessible to users from outside the building. These rooms will include movable seating and projection screens. To the extent possible, use of the auditorium should not disturb users of the smaller meeting rooms and vice versa.

ADMINISTRATIVE AND STAFF AREAS

The administrative and staff areas house the behind-the-scenes functions necessary to successful and efficient public service. Library staff and administrators are planners and managers of library resources. They work with one another and need facilities that emphasize departmental interaction. At the same time, they will need privacy and a quiet work area in order to conduct orderly planning. New technologies, such as a local area network and an integrated staff communication system with electronic mail, must be considered in the design. Communication should enhance access to administrative, secretarial, and financial services shared by all department heads.

Location of the area is also important to efficient operation. The area should be close to other library departments, yet acoustically and visually separate. Traffic from other departments or to frequently used areas should not be routed through work areas.

Staff Area

There are three elements to the staff area: a 750-square-foot lounge area, a separate 200-square-foot smoking room and a 100-square-foot retiring room. Restrooms should be nearby. The staff area should be near enough to the work areas so that staff can easily get to their jobs when needed but it should also be out of the main traffic flow so that library users do not wander into the area. There are no lockers or coat closets in this area; staff members have a room for coats and a lockable half or box locker in their primary work areas.

Administrative Offices

This area should be open and inviting while providing the staff privacy and a quiet place to work. It should be attractive yet efficient. It should also be easy for employees to get to and move around in, yet provide safety and security when they work late into the evening. Security can be improved with controllable access to the elevators, stair wells, and staff work areas. It should be possible to lock the administrative area at certain times. Because the staff must frequently work late and at times when the library is closed to the public, a separate staff entrance would improve staff productivity and security.

A small kitchen area with stove, refrigerator, and sink will be located near the board conference room. The staff lounge should be some distance from the administrative area. There will be two unisex restrooms for the administrative staff. The administrative area will have a small coat closet for guests and a larger closet for staff. The staff closet will have two umbrella stands and should be capable of holding thirty coats, while the visitor's closet will hold five or six coats.

A lobby area with atrium or clerestory, comfortable lounge chairs for waiting visitors, and greenery will make this an inviting, pleasant experience. Because there will not be a single reception area, the layout and signage should indicate a clear route to someone coming to this area for the first time.

Secretarial Office. Three staff members work closely together and share some resources. These key support personnel are the director's secretary, the assistant director's secretary (with primary responsibility for personnel), and the administrative assistant.

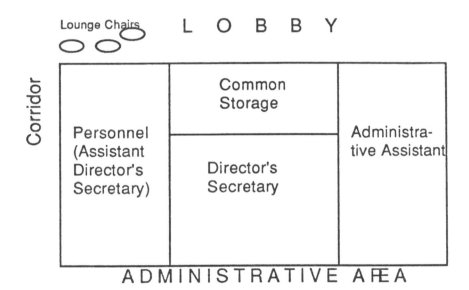

The design of these offices should reflect the need to articulate work flow and provide efficient access to materials in the common storage area. The area should use sound-dampening materials, possibly carpeted walls. The three-drawer files should be placed to provide unobtrusive, counter-height work stations. Natural light and task lighting are necessary in all parts of this area.

Director's Office. This office must be professional but elegant. There will be personal decorations, art, and sculpture. Natural lighting and a view of the city will add to the ambience. The design should include a secondary entrance/exit to this office.

Furnishings include an L-shaped desk and an executive chair with arms and casters. Task lighting will be available in all work areas of this office. There will be two substantial side chairs with arms and casters and a three-section sofa for visitors. Books and art work will be displayed on a floor-to-ceiling wall system. A conference area will either be in the director's office or adjacent to it. It will have a 5-foot-by-8-foot table and seven chairs with arms and casters. There will be task lighting over the table.

Assistant Director's Offices. There are two assistant directors, each with a separate office. These 200-square-foot offices should be pleasant and professional with operable windows. There will be an L-shaped desk and one swivel chair with arms and casters. One side chair will be provided for visitors. There will be a six-foot-high and 42 inch-wide book shelf behind the desk. Other furnishings include a pair of lounge chairs and a coffee table.

Board Conference Room. This pleasant, acoustically separate room will convey elegance and substance. There will be important works of art and a view of the city through a window behind the head of the table. It will assure privacy and confidence; there should not be a window in the conference room door.

The room will have a large Rudd System conference table and twenty upholstered stacking chairs. There will be adjustable task lighting on rheostats to augment the natural and ambiant light. There will be a telephone at a small side table, a tea trolley, clock, easel, and blackboard. One wall will have a tackable bulletin board and projection screen. There will be a coat closet with room for twenty coats, two umbrella stands and a separate eight-foot-by-two-foot deep storage area with 15-inch shelving.

Business Manager's Office. This bright, cheerful office should be located so that the manager can supervise and consult with the staff of the business office. It must also have easy access to the building superintendent, task and natural light, and operable windows. Furnishings include an L-shaped desk with computer and printer, two side chairs, a 5-foot credenza, and a work table with four chairs.

Business Office. There are eight work stations with room to add two more, each with a half locker or lockable cabinet. All work stations will be capable of holding computer systems. Furnishings include eight three-drawer file cabinets, a copy machine, and a fax machine. There are ten sections of single-faced wall shelving. A storage area for fourteen four-drawer file cabinets could be located nearby.

Building Superintendent's Office. The building superintendent should be near the business manager. This comfortable and efficient office will have a double pedestal desk and swivel chair with arms and casters for the superintendent and an L-shaped work station with printer stand for the assistant. There will be task and natural light and operable windows. Furnishings include two side chairs, two five-foot credenzas, a 4-foot-by-3-foot blue print cabinet, four three-drawer vertical file cabinets, and a 4-foot-by-6-foot work table.

Community Services Coordinator's Office. This 300-square-foot office will have a desk and two substantial side chairs for visitors. The community services coordinator's assistant will have a work station with printer stand. There will also be four three-drawer file cabinets and a 4-foot-by-6-foot layout table 36 inches high. This office should be located near the graphics and print shop.

Graphics and Print Shop

Posters, leaflets, brochures and other documents are created and repro-duced in this 600-square-foot shop. Task lighting for these functions is crucial. The area will require a hooded exhaust direct to the outside to vent solvent and spray fixative fumes. A sink and 42-inch-high electric outlets are also necessary. Garcy standards around the perimeter of the room will be used to mount a 30-inch wide counter at a 42-inch height. Shelving above and below the counter (also on the Garcy standards) will be used to shelve heavy paper supplies.

Storage

There will be adequate storage in closets and storerooms throughout the building, but there will be two large storage rooms where major supplies and little-used materials will be housed. Both storage areas will have locks. There is 600-square-foot storage area near the administrative suite to store daily supplies and lesser-used or dead files in fourteen four-drawer vertical file cabinets. The business office staff and the assistant director's secretary with personnel responsibilities will use these files most often. The room will have 15-inch industrial wall shelving on two walls.

Near the freight elevator and the dock is a 600-square-foot storage area where the bulk of the supplies are kept for the whole library system. It will have eighteen three-foot sections 90 inches high, 15-inch deep industrial wall shelving and nine three-foot sections of double-faced industrial shelving. There will also be a washer and dryer in this storage area. All shelving will be capable of holding heavy paper supplies.

Custodial Facilities

Custodians will have an office with desk, swivel chair, and side chair. There will also be a four-drawer vertical file cabinet. There will be a table for six and a sink, stove, and small refrigerator in a separate area. Nearby will be a custodial bathroom with shower stall.

There will be adequate custodial closets with 15-inch industrial shelving throughout the building. There will be closets with floor units on each level. An oversized trash compactor will be located near the loading dock. The freight elevator will be located near the dock and custodial offices and will be large enough for furniture and oversized items.

Loading Dock

A major library like the Yonkers Public Library receives thousands of books, magazines, newspapers, catalogs and other materials every day. Additionally, thousands of pounds of paper stock and equipment for the operation of the library come into the building on a regular basis. Library staff must be able to handle these materials efficiently and quickly.

In an unobtrusive location out of sight of the main entrance of the library, there will be a loading dock large enough for two vehicles. The dock should also be located away from primary work and public areas of the library so that noise and fumes from idling trucks do not disturb library users or staff. There will be adequate ventilation in the dock area. The dock will have a minimum overhead clearance of fourteen feet. The dock door will be radio controlled and will have an electronic safety eye. There will also be an intercom system for communication between the outside and the custodial staff office. There will be a drain in the floor of the loading dock.

SUMMARY

Implementation of this program will give the city of Yonkers an efficient library facility capable of providing modern information services well into the next century. It will be a focus of civic pride and a symbol of the community's hope and trust in future generations.

Bibliography

Robert B. Bechtel, Robert W. Marans, and William Michelson, editors. *Methods in Environmental and Behavioral Research*. New York: Van Nostrand Reinhold, 1987.

Robert B. Bechtel and R. K. Srivastava. *Post-Occupancy Evaluation of Housing*. Report submitted to the U.S. Department of Housing and Urban Development, 1978.

David Canter. "The Purposive Evaluation of Places: A Facet Approach." *Environment and Behavior* 15 (November 1983): 659–98.

David W. Carr. "Qualitative Meaning in Cultural Institutions." A paper presented at the annual meeting of the Association for Library and Information Science Education, Chicago, January 3, 1990.

Edwin S. Clay and Gailyn Hlavka. "Does This Building Work?" *Library Administration and Management* 1 (June 1987): 105–06.

John Daish, John Gray, David Kernohan, and Anne Salmond. "Post Occupancy Evaluation in New Zealand." *Design Studies* 3 (April 1982): 77–83.

John Daish, John Gray, David Kernohan, and Anne Salmond. "Post Occupancy Evaluations of Government Buildings." *Architectural Science Review* 26 (June 1983): 50–55.

Nolan A. Lushington and Willis N. Mills, Jr. *Libraries Designed for Users: A Planning Handbook*. Hamden, Conn.: Library Professional Publications, 1980.

McLure, Charles et al. *Planning and Role Setting for Public Libraries: A Manual of Options and Procedures*. Chicago: American Library Association, 1987.

Robert W. Marans and Kent F. Spreckelmeyer. *Evaluating Built Environments: A Behavioral Approach*. Ann Arbor: Institute for Social Research, University of Michigan, 1981.

Tom Peters. *Thriving on Chaos: Handbook for a Management Revolution.* New York: Knopf, 1988.

Robert S. Smith, compiler. *Checklist of Library Building Design Considerations.* American Library Association: LAMA/BES, Architecture for Public Libraries Committee, William W. Sannwald, chair. Chicago: American Library Association, July 1988.

Nancy Van House et al. *Output Measures for Public Libraries: A Manual of Standardized Procedures.* Chicago: American Library Association, 1987.

Eugene J. Webb, et al. *Unobtrusive Measures: Nonreactive Research in the Social Sciences.* Chicago: Rand McNally, 1966.

Carol H. Weiss. *Evaluation Research: Methods for Assessing Program Effectiveness.* Englewood Cliffs, N.J.: Prentice Hall, 1972.

Paul M. Wortman and Robert W. Marans. "Reviving Preevaluative Research: An Illustration from the Arts." *Evaluation Review* 11 (April 1987): 197–215.

Craig M. Zimring. "Evaluation of Designed Environments: Methods for Post-Occupancy Evaluation." In *Methods in Environmental and Behavioral Research,* ed. Robert B. Bechtel, Robert W. Marans, and William Michelson. New York: Van Nostrand Reinhold, 1987, pp. 270–300.

Craig M. Zimring and J. E. Reizenstien. "Post Occupancy Evaluation: An Overview." *Environment and Behavior* 12 (1982): 429–51.

Index